AND ALL FOR LOVE

The word 'love' is a short and simple one, and yet it is so complex and diverse in meaning. So many fine and terrible things are done in its name, but what is it exactly? Is it a 'many-splendored thing', as in the film and the romantic novel by Han Suyin? Or does it bring more tragedy than joy? Is it a burden, a prison, an agony to be endured?

It is all these things and more – unpredictable, wayward, uncertain. 'The course of true love never did run smooth,' wrote Shakespeare, and in these stories we find some of the torrents and whirlpools of love, the twists and turns that it takes. We have betrayal and vengeance, triumph and despair, fiery passion and quiet contentment. We have both devotion and denial, love as delight and as a terrible dilemma.

And at the end of these stories we might be no nearer knowing what love is. Perhaps the only answer lies in the words of Rabindranath Tagore, one of India's most famous poets:

Love is an endless mystery,
for it has nothing else to explain it.

OXFORD BOOKWORMS COLLECTION

Acknowledgements

The editors and publishers are grateful for permission to use the following copyright material:

'The Kimono' from *The Best of H. E. Bates* by H. E. BATES, published by Michael Joseph Ltd. Reprinted by permission of Laurence Pollinger Limited and the Estate of H. E. Bates.

'The Garden Party' by MAEVE BINCHY, first published in *Radio Times*. Copyright © Maeve Binchy 1995. Reprinted by permission of Christine Green Authors' Agent.

'A Shocking Accident' from *May We Borrow Your Husband?* by GRAHAM GREENE, first published by The Bodley Head. Copyright © Graham Greene 1986. Reprinted by permission of David Higham Associates Ltd.

'Ming's Biggest Prey' by PATRICIA HIGHSMITH. Copyright © Patricia Highsmith. Reprinted by permission of Tanja Howarth Literary Agency acting on behalf of Diogenes Verlag AG.

'A Painful Case' from *Dubliners* by JAMES JOYCE, first published 1914. Copyright © Estate of James Joyce. Reprinted by permission of the Estate of James Joyce.

'Mabel' from *The Complete Short Stories* by W. SOMERSET MAUGHAM, first published by William Heinemann Ltd 1951. Reprinted by permission of A. P. Watt Ltd on behalf of The Royal Literary Fund.

'The Children' from *Stories of the Waterfront* by JOHN MORRISON, published by Penguin Books Australia Ltd. Reprinted by permission of the publisher.

'Horrors of the Road' by FAY WELDON. Reprinted by permission of Curtis Brown/Edinburgh.

'The Legacy' by VIRGINIA WOOLF. Reprinted by permission of The Society of Authors as the Literary Representative of the Estate of Virginia Woolf.

AND ALL FOR LOVE ...

Short Stories

EDITED BY
Diane Mowat
Jennifer Bassett

SERIES ADVISERS
H. G. Widdowson
Jennifer Bassett

OXFORD UNIVERSITY PRESS
2001

OXFORD

UNIVERSITY PRESS

Great Clarendon Street, Oxford OX2 6DP

Oxford University Press is a department of the University of Oxford.
It furthers the University's objective of excellence in research, scholarship,
and education by publishing worldwide in

Oxford New York

Auckland Cape Town Dar es Salaam Hong Kong Karachi
Kuala Lumpur Madrid Melbourne Mexico City Nairobi
New Delhi Shanghai Taipei Toronto

With offices in

Argentina Austria Brazil Chile Czech Republic France Greece
Guatemala Hungary Italy Japan Poland Portugal Singapore
South Korea Switzerland Thailand Turkey Ukraine Vietnam

OXFORD and OXFORD ENGLISH are registered trade marks of
Oxford University Press in the UK and in certain other countries

ISBN-13: 978 0 19 422816 9

Printed in China

OXFORD BOOKWORMS
~ COLLECTION ~

FOREWORD

Texts of all kinds, including literary texts, are used as data for language teaching. They are designed or adapted and pressed into service to exemplify the language and provide practice in reading. These are commendable pedagogic purposes. They are not, however, what authors or readers of texts usually have in mind. The reason we read something is because we feel the writer has something of interest or significance to say and we only attend to the language to the extent that it helps us to understand what that might be. An important part of language learning is knowing how to adopt this normal reader role, how to use language to achieve meanings of significance to us, and so make texts our own.

The purpose of the *Oxford Bookworms Collection* is to encourage students of English to adopt this role. It offers samples of English language fiction, unabridged and unsimplified, which have been selected and presented to induce enjoyment, and to develop a sensitivity to the language through an appreciation of the literature. The intention is to stimulate students to find in fiction what Jane Austen found: 'the most thorough knowledge of human nature, the happiest delineation of its varieties, the liveliest effusions of wit and humour . . . conveyed to the world in the best chosen language.' *(Northanger Abbey)*

H. G. Widdowson
Series Adviser

OXFORD BOOKWORMS
~ COLLECTION ~

None of the texts has been abridged or simplified in any way, but each volume contains notes and questions to help students in their understanding and appreciation.

Before each story
- a short biographical note on the author
- an introduction to the theme and characters of the story

After each story
- NOTES

  Some words and phrases in the texts are marked with an asterisk*, and explanations for these are given in the notes. The expressions selected are usually cultural references or archaic and dialect words unlikely to be found in dictionaries. Other difficult words are not explained. This is because to do so might be to focus attention too much on the analysis of particular meanings, and to disrupt the natural reading process. Students should be encouraged by their engagement with the story to infer general and relevant meaning from context.

- DISCUSSION

  These are questions on the story's theme and characters, designed to stimulate class discussion or to encourage the individual reader to think about the story from different points of view.

- LANGUAGE FOCUS

  Some of these questions and tasks direct the reader's attention to particular features of language use or style; others focus on specific meanings and their significance in the story.

- ACTIVITIES

  These are suggestions for creative writing activities, to encourage readers to explore or develop the themes of the story in various imaginative ways.

- QUESTIONS FOR DISCUSSION OR WRITING

  These are questions (sometimes under the heading 'Ideas for Comparison Activities') with ideas for discussion or writing which compare and contrast a number of stories in the volume.

CURRENT TITLES

Contents

THE GARDEN PARTY

THE AUTHOR

Maeve Binchy was born in 1940 in Dublin. After school and university in Ireland she became a teacher and then a journalist. She has written plays for television and the stage, and is the author of many bestsellers, both novels and volumes of short stories. Among her novels are *Light a Penny Candle, Firefly Summer, The Copper Beech, The Glass Lake*, and *Tara Road*. Her novel *Circle of Friends* was made into a film in 1995. Maeve Binchy's books are affectionate pictures of the lives of ordinary people, and her stories concentrate on birth, friendship, marriage, death, and the small details of everyday life. She makes gentle fun of her characters, turning village gossip into art, and conveys a strong sense of the confusion of life, full of joys and sadnesses at the same time.

THE STORY

If a marriage fails, it can seem like the end of the world. A wife deserted for a younger woman, for example, can easily sink into depression and despair. But life goes on, and people recover – a cliché, but true. And as the Danish poet, Piet Hein, wrote: 'Things that don't actually kill you outright make you stronger.'

Helen, betrayed, deserted, and utterly forlorn, stares miserably out of the window of her new house at the garden next door. She sees no way of rebuilding her life into anything meaningful, until she meets her new neighbour, Mrs Kennedy, who has her own tale to tell – of a rather unusual strategy for survival . . .

THE GARDEN PARTY

Helen looked out the window at the garden next door. It was a mass of colour, mainly from bushes and small trees. No troublesome flowerbeds that would need endless weeding, nor were there paths that would have to have their edges trimmed, or rockeries where one thing might spill and crowd out another. Little brick paths wound through it and there were paved areas with tubs of plants around the garden seats; unlike her own garden which badly needed attention.

She had been told that her neighbour was a Mrs Kennedy, who had two placid cats and was known to be easy-going. Admittedly Helen had been told this by the estate agent who would hardly have warned her even if Mrs Kennedy had been one of the Brides of Dracula*.

Helen had been there for three days and she had not yet seen Mrs Kennedy. The two big cats spent almost all day asleep on the sunny garden seats. They looked so peaceful, Helen envied them. Dim creatures purring and dozing in the sunshine; someone to feed them at the end of every evening, birds to watch sleepily from a distance. How Helen wished that she too could have a life like that instead of sleepless nights, hours of anxiety, torrents of grief and regret. And now the whole nightmarish business of facing a new house, a new life, because Harry didn't love her any more, because he had found *real* love with this girl young enough to be his daughter. The girl who was pregnant with his child.

And Harry was so pleased to be a father. For fourteen years of their marriage he had told Helen that he wasn't ready for parenthood yet and that they were so complete in themselves they didn't need anyone else in their lives. Now, when she was thirty-six years old and he was approaching his fortieth birthday, he decided he would like to be a father. But he told her about the change of heart and direction only after he said that he was leaving her, and the mother of his child would be a nineteen-year-old.

Other people survived, but then other people could never have felt so betrayed, so shocked and so aimless now in life.

Her sisters lived far away in other cities; they were not a family given to writing or long telephone calls. And her friends? Helen knew only too well how easy it was to alienate your friends by weeping all night at their kitchen tables. Friends preferred to think you were coping, or trying to cope. Then they were supportive and practical and around. Friends could disappear into the woodwork if you cried on their shoulders as much as you wanted to.

So when Helen told people that she was going to move house, make a fresh start, everyone seemed pleased. A place with a garden, ideal they all said. Her sisters wrote and said she would find great consolation in digging the earth and planting and seeing things grow. Helen read their letters with mute rage.

She spent many hours of her first week in the new house staring aimlessly from the window and wondering about the unfairness of life. And then when she was least expecting it she saw Mrs Kennedy; much younger than she'd imagined – this woman barely looked ten years older than herself. She wore a rainbow-coloured skirt and a white T-shirt. She had a big black straw hat and smiled as she carried a tray of tea things to one of the two wooden tables in her garden.

Helen watched as she saw her neighbour sit down and stretch and close her eyes with pleasure in the afternoon sunshine. She was as languid and relaxed as one of the big sleepy cats.

As she watched, Helen heard the gate creak and two girls came in. One about sixteen, dark and attractive; one about six, a moppet with blonde curls. They flung themselves at the woman on the wooden seat.

'You were asleep, Debbie,' the older girl cried. 'We've finally caught you. This is what you do all day!'

'Poor Debbie, are you tired?' The six-year-old had climbed on Mrs Kennedy's lap and was hugging her.

Helen felt a wave of self-pity wash over her. She would never know anything like this. How could life have been so unfair? She wondered for a bit why they called the woman Debbie, but she could look and listen no longer. She sat down by a box of untouched china. She didn't know where she would store it, who would eat from it. No marvellous children would come and throw their arms around her calling her Helen.

The afternoon wore on. Helen unpacked one cup and one saucer and one plate. She couldn't live the rest of her life like this. But what were the alternatives? Harry was gone; he was not coming back. She wished she could get the woman next door out of her mind, but it was like probing a sore tooth.

When she heard a car draw up outside and a younger woman arrived to collect the girls, Helen was again at the window. The younger woman seemed to have trouble dragging the children away; there were still so many things to do. The teenager wanted to inspect the flowerbed, which was her very own, and examine the lupins. The little girl said she had to feed the cats. Then there was a final hug.

'Give our love to Granny,' said the teenager to Mrs Kennedy.

'Do you still have Granny, aren't you wonderful, Debbie,' said the younger woman: the girls' mother?

'I love Granny coming, we'll be making gingerbread and fudge tomorrow if you want to drop in.' Mrs Kennedy smiled encouragingly.

Immediately the girls said they would come, and Helen saw from her upstairs window a look of irritation cross the younger woman's face. She had to know who they were, these people who were acting out a play in the garden next door. There was wine unopened in her fridge. Helen wrapped it in tissue paper.

'I'm your new neighbour, Mrs Kennedy. I saw your friends or family leave just now so I thought I would come in and introduce myself. I'm Helen . . .' she began, and then burst into tears.

She didn't really remember the next bit, but she was sitting in the garden on the wooden seat with a cushion at her back. Debbie Kennedy had poured them two glasses of wine and produced some little bits of cheese and celery. They sat like old friends in the evening sun. And Debbie seemed to look into the distance at the sleeping cats as Helen wept the story of Harry and his betrayal. 'I can't go on, it's no use pretending.'

'I think you have to pretend one way or another, we all do. But the question is which way you pretend.' She was very matter of fact.

'How do you mean?' Helen had stopped crying.

'Well you could go one route and pretend nothing had changed and that you still thought he was wonderful, remain part of his life and take over the best bits . . .' Debbie spoke calmly. 'Or you could pretend that he is no longer part of your life and that you have forgotten him, and eventually, of course, you will. It will take time, but you will. It just depends which you think would bring you more peace, but both of them involve pretending.'

'I'll not forget him. I can't write it off, start again.' Helen felt the prickling tickling in her nose, and hoped she wasn't going to start crying again.

'Well then, don't forget him. Stick to him like a limpet, take over his life. I did,' Mrs Kennedy said, pouring them another glass of wine as she explained the story.

Her husband left her seven years ago for a woman who already had a ten-year-old daughter. A ready-made family, he called it. He left with a series of clichés: Debbie was a survivor, she had a good job, she wouldn't miss him, it would leave her time and space for the things she really loved. But Debbie had really loved her husband. She had been shattered as Helen was now. If grief could be measured, hers had been just as great. But she had decided not to lose him.

She had not been hostile to the woman with the ready-made family. She had been welcoming. She had offered to baby-sit for them. She had won the mind and heart of the girl who was now her husband's stepdaughter, Tina. She had moved to live near them; she was a presence in their lives. Her ex-husband thought she was a woman in a million. He sometimes came and talked with her in the garden. He lived in a place where the garden didn't flourish.

Debbie Kennedy had decided to make her successor's weaknesses her own strengths. Perhaps the new woman – she never spoke her name – was a tigress in bed; perhaps she was an intellectual giant; perhaps she flattered him more than Debbie had done. But Debbie still cooked better than she did. Debbie picked up his children from school and entertained them royally while the new woman was still at work. Debbie entertained her husband's mother regularly when the new woman had no time or inclination to do so. Debbie had arranged deviously that Tina should win two pedigree kittens in a competition when she knew the new woman was allergic to cats, and Debbie kept them, on loan, for Tina.

'It sounds like hard work,' Helen said, full of admiration.

'It's very hard work,' Debbie agreed. 'But then I was like you, I didn't think the day would come when I could ever live without him.'

'And now you could?'

'Oh yes, indeed I could. Now he actually bores me. Not totally but slightly. He's very predictable. You would know immediately how he will respond. I never thought the day would come . . .'

'So, if you're over him why don't you bow out? Live your own life?' Helen wondered.

'I can't now. I have too many other people that I love and who
love me. I have his mother; she never liked me much during the
marriage, but I'm like some kind of angel compared to the new
woman.'

'But surely . . .'

'No, I can't abandon her, she never did anyone any harm. She
didn't abandon me and divorce me, her son did. And I adore the
girls. And there are the cats. I only organised them out of spite, but
I love them now. I couldn't move on somewhere and abandon them
when they had served their purpose.

'And the garden: I realised that the secret was to have the
minimum to do, but to give the children a flowerbed each, and I
work on those secretly and feed whatever they plant, so they think
it's all their own work. It's a life, Helen, and I had no life the day
he said he was leaving.'

'But he's not the centre of it?'

'No, not now. He was when I needed it. Every single thing I did,
I did from some kind of vengeance, and it gave me a purpose to
my day.'

'I don't think I could do it. I mean it's not as if there were a ready-
made family. There's only a bump* and an awful nineteen-year-old,
and he doesn't have a mother, and the cat thing wouldn't work.'

'It's that or get out of his orbit completely. When do you go back
to work?'

'Next week.'

'Right, if you like, I'll ask the girls and Gran to help you unpack
tomorrow. It's much better with a few people there. We'll do a great
deal in an hour and a half . . .'

'But I can't.'

'Of course you can, and then, when you get back to work, have
a gardening party. Invite every one of your colleagues to lunch, say
that in return for two hours' gardening they'll have a great picnic.

Hire a huge trestle table for the day. I'll tell you what to tell them to plant and what to weed.'

'But I haven't decided which road to choose; whether to worm my way back into Harry's life or not.'

'You'll still need to unpack and to clear up that messy garden,' Debbie said.

They wouldn't talk about plans and strategies again. From now on they would not need to refer to the desperation of the one and the deviousness of the other. As the curtains went up at the windows, and the china was unpacked on to the shelves and into the cupboards, and the garden took shape, their lives would go on. Helen would make friends again. She would start with her colleagues in the bank who would view her differently after they had seen her as the host of a marvellous gardening party. Debbie's surrogate family would never know she had loved them initially as an act of revenge. It was good to have such solidarity established on a summer evening.

NOTES

Brides of Dracula　(p10)

a monster (Count Dracula was a vampire in Bram Stoker's novel *Dracula*; his brides were women he seduced and turned into vampires)

bump　(p15)

(informal) a reference to the new wife's pregnancy (i.e. the 'bump' in her body)

DISCUSSION

1 Revenge is usually thought of as a negative, destructive force. 'No revenge is more honourable than the one not taken,' a Spanish proverb says. Do you think Debbie's revenge can be seen like that? List the positive and negative features of all the things Debbie did, initially as acts of revenge.

2 Debbie was also deserted by her husband. What similarities were there between her situation and Helen's? Do you think Helen is likely to attempt a similar revenge? Would that, in your opinion, be a good idea? Why, or why not?

3 Describe the two routes that Debbie offers to Helen as ways forward out of her present situation. What other courses of action might deserted wives take? Do husbands deserted by their wives react in the same way? Do you think people generally have the same attitude towards an unfaithful wife as they do towards an unfaithful husband?

LANGUAGE FOCUS

1 Find these expressions in the story and explain what they mean.

Friends could disappear into the woodwork　(p11)
it was like probing a sore tooth　(p12)
I can't write it off, start again　(p13)
Stick to him like a limpet　(p13)
she was a woman in a million　(p14)
Perhaps the new woman [. . .] was a tigress in bed　(p14)
perhaps she was an intellectual giant　(p14)
if you're over him why don't you bow out?　(p14)
It's a life [. . .] and I had no life the day he said he was leaving　(p15)
or get out of his orbit completely　(p15)
whether to worm my way back into Harry's life　(p16)

2   *She wore a rainbow-coloured skirt and a white T-shirt. She had a big black straw hat . . .*
    This is the only time in the story that clothes are referred to. Why are they mentioned here, do you think?

3   *Helen saw from her upstairs window a look of irritation cross the younger woman's face.*
    What is the significance of that look?

4   Debbie tells Helen that her husband left with 'a series of clichés': '*You're a survivor; You have a good job; You won't miss me*', and so on. What purpose did these clichés serve for Mr Kennedy when he told his wife he was leaving her? Why do you think these expressions are described as clichés? Would they still feel like clichés if said to Debbie by a different person, for example, by a friend, or her mother?

ACTIVITIES

1   Helen decided to follow Debbie's suggestion to hold a gardening party. What other positive actions could she take to begin to rebuild her life? Write a paragraph of advice for her, as though for a 'problem page' in a magazine.

2   Imagine that you are one of Helen's sisters, writing one of the letters about the new house that Helen read with 'mute rage'. Use the information in the story to write the letter, full of hearty and insincere enthusiasm for the 'consolation' of gardening.

3   Mr Kennedy's second wife shows some irritation at her daughters' readiness to visit Debbie again the following day. Imagine that you are the girls' mother and write your diary entry for that day, describing how you feel about Debbie Kennedy and the girls' attitude towards her.

4   Is *The Garden Party* a good title for this story, do you think? Is it appropriate, and if so, in what way? What other suitable titles could you suggest?

ROMAN FEVER

THE AUTHOR

Edith Wharton was born in 1862 into a wealthy, upper-class New York family. She was educated privately at home and in 1885 married Edward Wharton. The marriage was not a success and in 1907 she left him to live in France, where she had a wide circle of writer and artist friends, including Henry James, the famous novelist. Wharton wrote novels, short stories, and several travel books. Her major novels include *Ethan Frome*, a tragic tale of passion and poverty, and *The Age of Innocence*, for which she won the Pulitzer Prize in 1920, the first woman to achieve this honour. A recurring theme of her writing was the struggle between social and personal fulfilment, which can often lead to tragedy. She died in France in 1937.

THE STORY

In the New York society of the early 1900s, the only career usually available to girls from upper-class families was to make a good marriage. Mothers kept a watchful eye on their daughters, and once a suitable young man had proposed, been accepted, and a formal engagement announced, there was an end to the matter. It was considered disgraceful behaviour to break off an engagement just because you had changed your mind.

Mrs Slade and Mrs Ansley, two upper-class American ladies, have known each other since childhood. Now both widows, each with one daughter, they meet by chance in Rome. The girls are out for the afternoon, and their mothers linger on a restaurant terrace, admiring the glories of ancient Rome spread out below them. As the evening light descends, they recall the courtship days of their youth. But it can be unwise to look too closely at the past . . .

Roman Fever

From the table at which they had been lunching two American ladies of ripe but well-cared-for middle age moved across the lofty terrace of the Roman restaurant and, leaning on its parapet, looked first at each other, and then down on the outspread glories of the Palatine and the Forum*, with the same expression of vague but benevolent approval.

As they leaned there a girlish voice echoed up gaily from the stairs leading to the court below. 'Well, come along, then,' it cried, not to them but to an invisible companion, 'and let's leave the young things to their knitting'; and a voice as fresh laughed back: 'Oh, look here, Babs, not actually *knitting*—' 'Well, I mean figuratively,' rejoined the first. 'After all, we haven't left our poor parents much else to do . . .' and at that point the turn of the stairs engulfed the dialogue.

The two ladies looked at each other again, this time with a tinge of smiling embarrassment, and the smaller and paler one shook her head and colored slightly.

'Barbara!' she murmured, sending an unheard rebuke after the mocking voice in the stairway.

The other lady, who was fuller, and higher in color, with a small determined nose supported by vigorous black eyebrows, gave a good-humored laugh. 'That's what our daughters think of us!'

Her companion replied by a deprecating gesture. 'Not of us individually. We must remember that. It's just the collective modern idea of Mothers. And you see—' Half-guiltily she drew from her handsomely mounted black handbag a twist of crimson silk run through by two fine knitting needles. 'One never knows,' she murmured. 'The new system* has certainly given us a good deal of time to kill; and sometimes I get tired just looking – even at this.'

Her gesture was now addressed to the stupendous scene at their feet.

The dark lady laughed again, and they both relapsed upon the view, contemplating it in silence, with a sort of diffused serenity which might have been borrowed from the spring effulgence of the Roman skies. The luncheon hour was long past, and the two had their end of the vast terrace to themselves. At its opposite extremity a few groups, detained by a lingering look at the outspread city, were gathering up guidebooks and fumbling for tips. The last of them scattered, and the two ladies were alone on the air-washed height.

'Well, I don't see why we shouldn't just stay here,' said Mrs Slade, the lady of the high color and energetic brows. Two derelict basket chairs stood near, and she pushed them into the angle of the parapet, and settled herself in one, her gaze upon the Palatine. 'After all, it's still the most beautiful view in the world.'

'It always will be, to me,' assented her friend Mrs Ansley, with so slight a stress on the 'me' that Mrs Slade, though she noticed it, wondered if it were not merely accidental, like the random underlinings of old-fashioned letter writers.

'Grace Ansley was always old-fashioned,' she thought; and added aloud, with a retrospective smile: 'It's a view we've both been familiar with for a good many years. When we first met here we were younger than our girls are now. You remember?'

'Oh, yes, I remember,' murmured Mrs Ansley, with the same undefinable stress. 'There's that headwaiter wondering,' she interpolated. She was evidently far less sure than her companion of herself and of her rights in the world.

'I'll cure him of wondering,' said Mrs Slade, stretching her hand toward a bag as discreetly opulent-looking as Mrs Ansley's. Signing to the headwaiter, she explained that she and her friend were old lovers of Rome, and would like to spend the end of the afternoon looking down on the view – that is, if it did not disturb the service? The headwaiter, bowing over her gratuity, assured her that the ladies were most welcome, and would be still more so if they would condescend to remain for dinner. A full-moon night, they would remember . . .

Mrs Slade's black brows drew together, as though references to the moon were out of place and even unwelcome. But she smiled away her frown as the headwaiter retreated. 'Well, why not? We might do worse. There's no knowing, I suppose, when the girls will be back. Do you even know back from *where?* I don't!'

Mrs Ansley again colored slightly. 'I think those young Italian aviators we met at the Embassy invited them to fly to Tarquinia for tea. I suppose they'll want to wait and fly back by moonlight.'

'Moonlight – moonlight! What a part it still plays. Do you suppose they're as sentimental as we were?'

'I've come to the conclusion that I don't in the least know what they are,' said Mrs Ansley. 'And perhaps we didn't know much more about each other.'

'No; perhaps we didn't.'

Her friend gave her a shy glance. 'I never should have supposed you were sentimental, Alida.'

'Well, perhaps I wasn't.' Mrs Slade drew her lids together in retrospect; and for a few moments the two ladies, who had been intimate since childhood, reflected how little they knew each other. Each one, of course, had a label ready to attach to the other's name; Mrs Delphin Slade*, for instance, would have told herself, or anyone who asked her, that Mrs Horace Ansley*, twenty-five years ago, had been exquisitely lovely – no, you wouldn't believe it, would you? . . . though, of course, still charming, distinguished . . . Well, as a girl she had been exquisite; far more beautiful than her daughter Barbara, though certainly Babs, according to the new standards at any rate, was more effective – had more *edge*, as they say. Funny where she got it, with those two nullities as parents. Yes; Horace Ansley was – well, just the duplicate of his wife. Museum specimens of old New York. Good-looking, irreproachable, exemplary. Mrs Slade and Mrs Ansley had lived opposite each other – actually as well as figuratively – for years. When the drawing-room curtains in No. 20 East 73rd Street were renewed, No. 23, across the way, was always aware of it. And of all the movings, buyings, travels, anniversaries, illnesses – the tame chronicle of an estimable pair. Little of it escaped Mrs Slade. But she had grown bored with it by the time her husband made his big *coup* in Wall Street*, and when they bought in upper Park Avenue had already begun to think: 'I'd rather live opposite a speakeasy* for a change; at least one might see it raided.' The idea of seeing Grace raided was so amusing that (before the move) she launched it at a women's lunch. It made a hit, and went the rounds – she sometimes wondered if it had crossed the street, and reached Mrs Ansley. She hoped not, but didn't much mind. Those were the days when respectability was at a discount, and it did the irreproachable no harm to laugh at them a little.

A few years later, and not many months apart, both ladies lost their husbands. There was an appropriate exchange of wreaths and condolences, and a brief renewal of intimacy in the half-shadow of their mourning; and now, after another interval, they had run across each other in Rome, at the same hotel, each of them the modest appendage of a salient daughter. The similarity of their lot had again drawn them together, lending itself to mild jokes, and the mutual confession that, if in old days it must have been tiring to 'keep up' with daughters, it was now, at times, a little dull not to.

No doubt, Mrs Slade reflected, she felt her unemployment more than poor Grace ever would. It was a big drop from being the wife of Delphin Slade to being his widow. She had always regarded herself (with a certain conjugal pride) as his equal in social gifts, as contributing her full share to the making of the exceptional couple they were: but the difference after his death was irremediable. As the wife of the famous corporation lawyer, always

with an international case or two on hand, every day brought its
exciting and unexpected obligation: the impromptu entertaining of
eminent colleagues from abroad, the hurried dashes on legal
business to London, Paris or Rome, where the entertaining was so
handsomely reciprocated; the amusement of hearing in her wake:
'What, that handsome woman with the good clothes and the eyes
is Mrs Slade – *the* Slade's wife? Really? Generally the wives of
celebrities are such frumps.'

Yes; being *the* Slade's widow was a dullish business after that. In
living up to such a husband all her faculties had been engaged; now
she had only her daughter to live up to, for the son who seemed to
have inherited his father's gifts had died suddenly in boyhood. She
had fought through that agony because her husband was there, to
be helped and to help; now, after the father's death, the thought of
the boy had become unbearable. There was nothing left but to
mother her daughter; and dear Jenny was such a perfect daughter
that she needed no excessive mothering. 'Now with Babs Ansley I
don't know that I *should* be so quiet,' Mrs Slade sometimes half-
enviously reflected; but Jenny, who was younger than her brilliant
friend, was that rare accident, an extremely pretty girl who
somehow made youth and prettiness seem as safe as their absence.
It was all perplexing – and to Mrs Slade a little boring. She wished
that Jenny would fall in love – with the wrong man, even; that she
might have to be watched, out-maneuvered, rescued. And instead,
it was Jenny who watched her mother, kept her out of drafts, made
sure that she had taken her tonic . . .

Mrs Ansley was much less articulate than her friend, and her
mental portrait of Mrs Slade was slighter, and drawn with fainter
touches. 'Alida Slade's awfully brilliant; but not as brilliant as she
thinks,' would have summed it up; though she would have added,
for the enlightenment of strangers, that Mrs Slade had been an
extremely dashing girl; much more so than her daughter, who was

pretty, of course, and clever in a way, but had none of her mother's
– well, 'vividness', someone had once called it. Mrs Ansley would
take up current words like this, and cite them in quotation marks,
as unheard-of audacities. No; Jenny was not like her mother.
Sometimes Mrs Ansley thought Alida Slade was disappointed; on
the whole she had had a sad life. Full of failures and mistakes; Mrs
Ansley had always been rather sorry for her . . .

So these two ladies visualized each other, each through the wrong
end of her little telescope.

* * *

For a long time they continued to sit side by side without speaking.
It seemed as though, to both, there was a relief in laying down their
somewhat futile activities in the presence of the vast Memento
Mori* which faced them. Mrs Slade sat quite still, her eyes fixed
on the golden slope of the Palace of the Caesars, and after a while
Mrs Ansley ceased to fidget with her bag, and she too sank into
meditation. Like many intimate friends, the two ladies had never
before had occasion to be silent together, and Mrs Ansley was
slightly embarrassed by what seemed, after so many years, a new
stage in their intimacy, and one with which she did not yet know
how to deal.

Suddenly the air was full of that deep clangor of bells which
periodically covers Rome with a roof of silver. Mrs Slade glanced at
her wristwatch. 'Five o'clock already,' she said, as though surprised.

Mrs Ansley suggested interrogatively: 'There's bridge at the
Embassy at five.' For a long time Mrs Slade did not answer. She
appeared to be lost in contemplation, and Mrs Ansley thought the
remark had escaped her. But after a while she said, as if speaking
out of a dream: 'Bridge, did you say? Not unless you want to . . .
But I don't think I will, you know.'

'Oh, no,' Mrs Ansley hastened to assure her. 'I don't care to at all. It's so lovely here; and so full of old memories, as you say.' She settled herself in her chair, and almost furtively drew forth her knitting. Mrs Slade took sideway note of this activity, but her own beautifully cared-for hands remained motionless on her knee.

'I was just thinking,' she said slowly, 'what different things Rome stands for to each generation of travelers. To our grandmothers, Roman fever; to our mothers, sentimental dangers – how we used to be guarded! – to our daughters, no more dangers than the middle of Main Street. They don't know it – but how much they're missing!'

The long golden light was beginning to pale, and Mrs Ansley lifted her knitting a little closer to her eyes. 'Yes, how we were guarded!'

'I always used to think,' Mrs Slade continued, 'that our mothers had a much more difficult job than our grandmothers. When Roman fever stalked the streets it must have been comparatively easy to gather in the girls at the danger hour; but when you and I were young, with such beauty calling us, and the spice of disobedience thrown in, and no worse risk than catching cold during the cool hour after sunset, the mothers used to be put to it to keep us in – didn't they?'

She turned again toward Mrs Ansley, but the latter had reached a delicate point in her knitting. 'One, two, three – slip two; yes, they must have been,' she assented, without looking up.

Mrs Slade's eyes rested on her with a deepened attention. 'She can knit – in the face of *this*! How like her . . .'

Mrs Slade leaned back, brooding, her eyes ranging from the ruins which faced her to the long green hollow of the Forum, the fading glow of the church fronts beyond it, and the outlying immensity of the Colosseum*. Suddenly she thought: 'It's all very well to say that our girls have done away with sentiment and moonlight. But if Babs Ansley isn't out to catch that young aviator – the one who's a Marchese* – then I don't know anything. And Jenny has no chance beside her. I know that too. I wonder if that's why Grace Ansley likes the two girls to go everywhere together? My poor Jenny as a foil—!' Mrs Slade gave a hardly audible laugh, and at the sound Mrs Ansley dropped her knitting.

'Yes—?'

'I – oh, nothing. I was only thinking how your Babs carries everything before her. That Campolieri boy is one of the best matches in Rome. Don't look so innocent, my dear – you know he is. And I was wondering, ever so respectfully, you understand . . . wondering how two such exemplary characters as you and Horace had managed to produce anything quite so dynamic.' Mrs Slade laughed again, with a touch of asperity.

Mrs Ansley's hands lay inert across her needles. She looked straight out at the great accumulated wreckage of passion and splendor at her feet. But her small profile was almost expressionless. At length she said: 'I think you overrate Babs, my dear.'

Mrs Slade's tone grew easier. 'No; I don't. I appreciate her. And perhaps envy you. Oh, my girl's perfect; if I were a chronic invalid I'd – well, I think I'd rather be in Jenny's hands. There must be times . . . but there! I always wanted a brilliant daughter . . . and never quite understood why I got an angel instead.'

Mrs Ansley echoed her laugh in a faint murmur. 'Babs is an angel too.'

'Of course – of course! But she's got rainbow wings. Well, they're wandering by the sea with their young men; and here we sit . . . and it all brings back the past a little too acutely.'

Mrs Ansley had resumed her knitting. One might almost have imagined (if one had known her less well, Mrs Slade reflected) that, for her also, too many memories rose from the lengthening shadows of those august ruins. But no; she was simply absorbed in her work. What was there for her to worry about? She knew that Babs would almost certainly come back engaged to the extremely eligible Campolieri. 'And she'll sell the New York house, and settle down near them in Rome, and never be in their way . . . she's much too tactful. But she'll have an excellent cook, and just the right people in for bridge and cocktails . . . and a perfectly peaceful old age among her grandchildren.'

Mrs Slade broke off this prophetic flight with a recoil of self-disgust. There was no one of whom she had less right to think unkindly than of Grace Ansley. Would she never cure herself of envying her? Perhaps she had begun too long ago.

She stood up and leaned against the parapet, filling her troubled eyes with the tranquilizing magic of the hour. But instead of tranquilizing her the sight seemed to increase her exasperation. Her gaze turned toward the Colosseum. Already its golden flank was drowned in purple shadow, and above it the sky curved crystal clear, without light or color. It was the moment when afternoon and evening hang balanced in mid-heaven.

Mrs Slade turned back and laid her hand on her friend's arm. The gesture was so abrupt that Mrs Ansley looked up, startled.

'The sun's set. You're not afraid, my dear?'

'Afraid—?'

'Of Roman fever or pneumonia? I remember how ill you were that winter. As a girl you had a very delicate throat, hadn't you?'

'Oh, we're all right up here. Down below, in the Forum, it does get deathly cold, all of a sudden . . . but not here.'

'Ah, of course you know because you had to be so careful.' Mrs Slade turned back to the parapet. She thought: 'I must make one more effort not to hate her.' Aloud she said: 'Whenever I look at the Forum from up here, I remember that story about a great-aunt of yours, wasn't she? A dreadfully wicked great-aunt?'

'Oh, yes; great-aunt Harriet. The one who was supposed to have sent her young sister out to the Forum after sunset to gather a night-blooming flower for her album. All our great-aunts and grandmothers used to have albums of dried flowers.'

Mrs Slade nodded. 'But she really sent her because they were in love with the same man—'

'Well, that was the family tradition. They said Aunt Harriet confessed it years afterward. At any rate, the poor little sister caught the fever and died. Mother used to frighten us with the story when we were children.'

'And you frightened *me* with it, that winter when you and I were here as girls. The winter I was engaged to Delphin.'

Mrs Ansley gave a faint laugh. 'Oh, did I? Really frightened you? I don't believe you're easily frightened.'

'Not often; but I was then. I was easily frightened because I was too happy. I wonder if you know what that means?'

'I – yes . . .' Mrs Ansley faltered.

'Well, I suppose that was why the story of your wicked aunt made such an impression on me. And I thought: "There's no more Roman fever, but the Forum is deathly cold after sunset – especially after a hot day. And the Colosseum's even colder and damper."'

'The Colosseum—?'

'Yes. It wasn't easy to get in, after the gates were locked for the night. Far from easy. Still, in those days it could be managed; it *was* managed, often. Lovers met there who couldn't meet elsewhere. You knew that?'

'I – I dare say. I don't remember.'

'You don't remember? You don't remember going to visit some ruins or other one evening, just after dark, and catching a bad chill? You were supposed to have gone to see the moon rise. People always said that expedition was what caused your illness.'

There was a moment's silence; then Mrs Ansley rejoined: 'Did they? It was all so long ago.'

'Yes. And you got well again – so it didn't matter. But I suppose it struck your friends – the reason given for your illness, I mean – because everybody knew you were so prudent on account of your throat, and your mother took such care of you . . . You *had* been out late sight-seeing, hadn't you, that night?'

'Perhaps I had. The most prudent girls aren't always prudent. What made you think of it now?'

Mrs Slade seemed to have no answer ready. But after a moment she broke out: 'Because I simply can't bear it any longer—!'

Mrs Ansley lifted her head quickly. Her eyes were wide and very pale. 'Can't bear what?'

'Why – your not knowing that I've always known why you went.'

'Why I went—?'

'Yes. You think I'm bluffing, don't you? Well, you went to meet the man I was engaged to – and I can repeat every word of the letter that took you there.'

While Mrs Slade spoke Mrs Ansley had risen unsteadily to her feet. Her bag, her knitting and gloves, slid in a panic-stricken heap to the ground. She looked at Mrs Slade as though she were looking at a ghost.

'No, no – don't,' she faltered out.

'Why not? Listen, if you don't believe me. "My one darling, things can't go on like this. I must see you alone. Come to the Colosseum immediately after dark tomorrow. There will be somebody to let you in. No one whom you need fear will suspect" – but perhaps you've forgotten what the letter said?'

Mrs Ansley met the challenge with an unexpected composure. Steadying herself against the chair she looked at her friend, and replied: 'No; I know it by heart too.'

'And the signature? "Only *your* D.S." Was that it? I'm right, am I? That was the letter that took you out that evening after dark?'

Mrs Ansley was still looking at her. It seemed to Mrs Slade that a slow struggle was going on behind the voluntarily controlled mask of her small quiet face. 'I shouldn't have thought she had herself so well in hand,' Mrs Slade reflected, almost resentfully. But at this moment Mrs Ansley spoke. 'I don't know how you knew. I burnt that letter at once.'

'Yes; you would, naturally – you're so prudent!' The sneer was open now. 'And if you burnt the letter you're wondering how on earth I know what was in it. That's it, isn't it?'

Mrs Slade waited, but Mrs Ansley did not speak.

'Well, my dear, I know what was in that letter because I wrote it!'

'You wrote it?'

'Yes.'

The two women stood for a minute staring at each other in the last golden light. Then Mrs Ansley dropped back into her chair. 'Oh,' she murmured, and covered her face with her hands.

Mrs Slade waited nervously for another word or movement. None came, and at length she broke out: 'I horrify you.'

Mrs Ansley's hands dropped to her knee. The face they uncovered was streaked with tears. 'I wasn't thinking of you. I was thinking – it was the only letter I ever had from him!'

'And I wrote it. Yes; I wrote it! But I was the girl he was engaged to. Did you happen to remember that?'

Mrs Ansley's head drooped again. 'I'm not trying to excuse myself . . . I remembered . . .'

'And still you went?'

'Still I went.'

Mrs Slade stood looking down on the small bowed figure at her side. The flame of her wrath had already sunk, and she wondered why she had ever thought there would be any satisfaction in inflicting so purposeless a wound on her friend. But she had to justify herself.

'You do understand? I'd found out – and I hated you, hated you. I knew you were in love with Delphin – and I was afraid; afraid of you, of your quiet ways, your sweetness . . . your . . . well, I wanted you out of the way, that's all. Just for a few weeks; just till I was sure of him. So in a blind fury I wrote that letter . . . I don't know why I'm telling you now.'

'I suppose,' said Mrs Ansley slowly, 'it's because you've always gone on hating me.'

'Perhaps. Or because I wanted to get the whole thing off my mind.' She paused. 'I'm glad you destroyed the letter. Of course I never thought you'd die.'

Mrs Ansley relapsed into silence, and Mrs Slade, leaning above her, was conscious of a strange sense of isolation, of being cut off from the warm current of human communion. 'You think me a monster!'

'I don't know . . . It was the only letter I had, and you say he didn't write it?'

'Ah, how you care for him still!'

'I cared for that memory,' said Mrs Ansley.

Mrs Slade continued to look down on her. She seemed physically reduced by the blow – as if, when she got up, the wind might scatter her like a puff of dust. Mrs Slade's jealousy suddenly leapt up again at the sight. All these years the woman had been living on that letter. How she must have loved him, to treasure the mere memory of its ashes! The letter of the man her friend was engaged to. Wasn't it she who was the monster?

'You tried your best to get him away from me, didn't you? But you failed; and I kept him. That's all.'

'Yes. That's all.'

'I wish now I hadn't told you. I'd no idea you'd feel about it as you do; I thought you'd be amused. It all happened so long ago, as you say; and you must do me the justice to remember that I had no reason to think you'd ever taken it seriously. How could I, when you were married to Horace Ansley two months afterward? As soon as you could get out of bed your mother rushed you off to Florence and married you. People were rather surprised – they wondered at its being done so quickly; but I thought I knew. I had an idea you did it out of *pique* – to be able to say you'd got ahead of Delphin and me. Girls have such silly reasons for doing the most serious things. And your marrying so soon convinced me that you'd never really cared.'

'Yes. I suppose it would,' Mrs Ansley assented.

The clear heaven overhead was emptied of all its gold. Dusk spread over it, abruptly darkening the Seven Hills. Here and there lights began to twinkle through the foliage at their feet. Steps were coming and going on the deserted terrace – waiters looking out of the doorway at the head of the stairs, then reappearing with trays and napkins and flasks of wine. Tables were moved, chairs straightened. A feeble string of electric lights flickered out. Some vases of faded flowers were carried away, and brought back replenished. A stout lady in a dust coat suddenly appeared, asking in broken Italian if anyone had seen the elastic band which held together her tattered Baedeker*. She poked with her stick under the table at which she had lunched, the waiters assisting.

The corner where Mrs Slade and Mrs Ansley sat was still shadowy and deserted. For a long time neither of them spoke. At length Mrs Slade began again: 'I suppose I did it as a sort of joke—'

'A joke?'

'Well, girls are ferocious sometimes, you know. Girls in love especially. And I remember laughing to myself all that evening at the idea that you were waiting around there in the dark, dodging out of sight, listening for every sound, trying to get in – Of course I was upset when I heard you were so ill afterward.'

Mrs Ansley had not moved for a long time. But now she turned slowly toward her companion. 'But I didn't wait. He'd arranged everything. He was there. We were let in at once,' she said.

Mrs Slade sprang up from her leaning position. 'Delphin there? They let you in? – Ah, now you're lying!' she burst out with violence.

Mrs Ansley's voice grew clearer, and full of surprise. 'But of course he was there. Naturally he came—'

'Came? How did he know he'd find you there? You must be raving!'

Mrs Ansley hesitated, as though reflecting. 'But I answered the letter. I told him I'd be there. So he came.'

Mrs Slade flung her hands up to her face. 'Oh, God – you answered! I never thought of your answering . . .'

'It's odd you never thought of it, if you wrote the letter.'

'Yes. I was blind with rage.'

Mrs Ansley rose, and drew her fur scarf about her. 'It is cold here. We'd better go . . . I'm sorry for you,' she said, as she clasped the fur about her throat.

The unexpected words sent a pang through Mrs Slade. 'Yes; we'd better go.' She gathered up her bag and cloak. 'I don't know why you should be sorry for me,' she muttered.

Mrs Ansley stood looking away from her toward the dusky secret mass of the Colosseum. 'Well – because I didn't have to wait that night.'

Mrs Slade gave an unquiet laugh. 'Yes; I was beaten there. But I oughtn't to begrudge it to you, I suppose. At the end of all these years. After all, I had everything; I had him for twenty-five years. And you had nothing but that one letter that he didn't write.'

Mrs Ansley was again silent. At length she turned toward the door of the terrace. She took a step, and turned back, facing her companion.

'I had Barbara,' she said, and began to move ahead of Mrs Slade toward the stairway.

Notes

the Palatine, the Forum   (p20)

the Palatine is one of the seven hills of Rome; the Forum is the ruins of what was once the commercial and political centre of ancient Rome

the new system   (p20)

possibly a reference to the 'modern idea of Mothers', in that mothers no longer spent a lot of their time monitoring and supervising their daughters' social lives

Mrs Delphin Slade, Mrs Horace Ansley   (p22)

the custom of referring to a married woman by both her husband's surname *and* his forename used to be quite normal, but is less so now

Wall Street   (p23)

the financial centre of New York

speakeasy   (p23)

an illegal club or shop where alcoholic drink could be bought during Prohibition (the years 1920–33, when alcohol was banned in the USA)

Memento Mori   (p25)

a warning or reminder of death (a Latin phrase meaning 'remember you must die')

the Colosseum   (p26)

one of the most famous ruins of ancient Rome, an open-air theatre which could seat 50,000 people

Marchese   (p26)

the title of an Italian nobleman

Baedeker   (p33)

a famous guidebook used by travellers at this time

Discussion

1 What effect do you think Mrs Ansley's revelation will have on Mrs Slade? The author describes them as 'intimate friends', but what is the nature of their friendship? Do you think that the friendship, such as it is, will survive after these revelations?

2 Which of the two women do you feel more sympathy for? Why? The quiet Mrs Ansley gets her revenge on Mrs Slade in the end. Do you think she was justified in doing that? In your opinion, are there any situations in which revenge can be justified?

Language Focus

1 The word 'fever' in the story's title has two meanings, one literal and
   one figurative. What are they? Do you think *Roman Fever* is a good title
   for this story? What other titles could you suggest?

2 *Mrs Ansley's hands lay inert across her needles. She looked straight out
   at the great accumulated wreckage of passion and splendor at her feet.
   But her small profile was almost expressionless. At length . . .*
   Why do you think Mrs Ansley stops knitting at this moment? And what
   is all this about 'accumulated wreckage'? And why the pause?

3 Explain, in simple everyday English, the following expressions:

   a good deal of time to kill (p20)
   It made a hit, and went the rounds (p23)
   they had run across each other in Rome (p23)
   In living up to such a husband (p24)
   the spice of disobedience thrown in (p26)
   how your Babs carries everything before her (p27)
   I shouldn't have thought she had herself so well in hand (p31)

Activities

1 The story is told mostly from Mrs Slade's viewpoint, and we are given
   only a few insights into Mrs Ansley's thoughts. During the conversation
   about the letter her responses often show some hesitation, as though
   she were having an internal debate with herself. Imagine that you are
   Mrs Ansley and write down your thoughts as you listen to Mrs Slade.

2 What clues are we given to the characters of both daughters? Suppose
   that after the end of the story both mothers decide to tell their respective
   daughters the truth about Barbara's parentage. Write two short
   dialogues, one for each mother and daughter, giving the reaction you
   think each daughter might have on discovering the truth.

3 Mrs Ansley's last three words change most of our assumptions about
   that Roman night twenty-five years ago, but, tantalisingly, we are told
   very little about the attitudes of the two illicit lovers. Did Delphin want
   to break his engagement to Alida and marry Grace, or did he feel that
   he should honourably keep his engagement? Did Grace try to persuade
   Delphin to marry her or not? Write a new ending for the story, describing
   what Delphin and Grace said to each other on that night.

THE LEGACY

THE AUTHOR

Virginia Woolf was born in London in 1882, where she lived for most of her life and was a member of the avant-garde 'Bloomsbury Group'. In 1912 she married Leonard Woolf, with whom she founded the Hogarth Press in 1917. Her first two novels were realistic in form, but *Jacob's Room* (1922) was unusual for its indirect narration and poetic impressionism. Her experimental techniques in other famous novels – *Mrs Dalloway, To the Lighthouse, The Waves,* and *Between the Acts* – have greatly influenced modern fiction. She was also a distinguished literary critic and journalist; the long essay *A Room of One's Own* (1929) is a classic of the feminist movement. Throughout her life she suffered from bouts of mental illness, and the last attack in 1941 caused her to take her own life.

THE STORY

It is possible to live with someone for years, and to think that you know everything about them. You might be right; on the other hand, that person may have hidden depths, secrets that never see the light of day. Perhaps it is better that way. There is an old saying that 'What the eye doesn't see, the heart doesn't grieve over.'

Gilbert Clandon is a prominent politician, a successful man with a good understanding of his own worth. His wife Angela recently met a tragic death in an accident, and now Gilbert sits at home, waiting for her secretary, Sissy Miller, who is coming to collect the brooch which is her legacy from Angela. On the desk behind Gilbert sits his own legacy from Angela, fifteen leather-bound volumes – the diary that she kept during all the years of their marriage, and which she would never allow him to read . . .

THE LEGACY

'For Sissy Miller.' Gilbert Clandon, taking up the pearl brooch that lay among a litter of rings and brooches on a little table in his wife's drawing-room, read the inscription: 'For Sissy Miller, with my love.'

It was like Angela to have remembered even Sissy Miller, her secretary. Yet how strange it was, Gilbert Clandon thought once more, that she had left everything in such order – a little gift of some sort for every one of her friends. It was as if she had foreseen her death. Yet she had been in perfect health when she left the house that morning, six weeks ago; when she stepped off the kerb in Piccadilly* and the car had killed her.

He was waiting for Sissy Miller. He had asked her to come; he owed her, he felt, after all the years she had been with them, this token of consideration. Yes, he went on, as he sat there waiting, it was strange that Angela had left everything in such order. Every friend had been left some little token of her affection. Every ring, every necklace, every little Chinese box – she had a passion for little boxes – had a name on it. And each had some memory for him. This he had given her; this – the enamel dolphin with the ruby eyes – she had pounced upon one day in a back street in Venice. He could remember her little cry of delight. To him of course, she had left nothing in particular, unless it were her diary. Fifteen little volumes, bound in green leather, stood behind him on her writing table. Ever since they were married, she had kept a diary. Some of their very few – he could not call them quarrels, say tiffs – had been about that diary. When he came in and found her writing, she always shut it or put her hand over it. 'No, no, no,' he could hear her say, 'After I'm dead – perhaps.' So she had left it him, as her legacy. It was the only thing they had not shared when she was alive. But he had always taken it for granted that she would outlive him. If only she had stopped one moment, and had thought what she was doing, she would be alive now. But she had stepped straight off the kerb, the driver of the car had said at the inquest. She had given him no chance to pull up . . . Here the sound of voices in the hall interrupted him.

'Miss Miller, Sir,' said the maid.

She came in. He had never seen her alone in his life, nor, of course, in tears. She was terribly distressed, and no wonder. Angela had been much more to her than an employer. She had been a friend. To himself, he thought, as he pushed a chair for her and asked her to sit down, she was scarcely distinguishable from any other woman of her kind. There were thousands of Sissy Millers – drab little women in black carrying attaché cases. But Angela, with her genius for sympathy, had discovered all sorts of qualities in Sissy Miller. She was the soul of discretion; so silent; so trustworthy, one could tell her anything, and so on.

Miss Miller could not speak at first. She sat there dabbing her eyes with her pocket handkerchief. Then she made an effort.

'Pardon me, Mr Clandon,' she said.

He murmured. Of course he understood. It was only natural. He could guess what his wife had meant to her.

'I've been so happy here,' she said, looking round. Her eyes rested on the writing table behind him. It was here they had worked – she and Angela. For Angela had her share of the duties that fall to the lot of a prominent politician's wife. She had been the greatest help to him in his career. He had often seen her and Sissy sitting at that table – Sissy at the typewriter, taking down letters from her dictation. No doubt Miss Miller was thinking of that, too. Now all he had to do was to give her the brooch his wife had left her. A rather incongruous gift it seemed. It might have been better to have left her a sum of money, or even the typewriter. But there it was –

'For Sissy Miller, with my love.' And, taking the brooch, he gave it her with the little speech that he had prepared. He knew, he said, that she would value it. His wife had often worn it . . . And she replied, as she took it almost as if she too had prepared a speech, that it would always be a treasured possession . . . She had, he supposed, other clothes upon which a pearl brooch would not look quite so incongruous. She was wearing the little black coat and skirt that seemed the uniform of her profession. Then he remembered – she was in mourning, of course. She, too, had had her tragedy – a brother, to whom she was devoted, had died only a week or two before Angela. In some accident was it? He could not remember – only Angela telling him. Angela, with her genius for sympathy, had been terribly upset. Meanwhile Sissy Miller had risen. She was putting on her gloves. Evidently she felt that she ought not to intrude. But he could not let her go without saying something about her future. What were her plans? Was there any way in which he could help her?

She was gazing at the table, where she had sat at her typewriter, where the diary lay. And, lost in her memories of Angela, she did not at once answer his suggestion that he should help her. She seemed for a moment not to understand. So he repeated:

'What are your plans, Miss Miller?'

'My plans? Oh, that's all right, Mr Clandon,' she exclaimed. 'Please don't bother yourself about me.'

He took her to mean that she was in no need of financial assistance. It would be better, he realized, to make any suggestion of that kind in a letter. All he could do now was to say as he pressed her hand, 'Remember, Miss Miller, if there's any way in which I can help you, it will be a pleasure . . .' Then he opened the door. For a moment, on the threshold, as if a sudden thought had struck her, she stopped.

'Mr Clandon,' she said, looking straight at him for the first time, and for the first time he was struck by the expression, sympathetic yet searching, in her eyes. 'If at any time,' she continued, 'there's anything I can do to help you, remember, I shall feel it, for your wife's sake, a pleasure . . .'

With that she was gone. Her words and the look that went with them were unexpected. It was almost as if she believed, or hoped, that he would need her. A curious, perhaps a fantastic idea occurred to him as he returned to his chair. Could it be, that during all those years when he had scarcely noticed her, she, as the novelists say, had entertained a passion for him? He caught his own reflection in the glass as he passed. He was over fifty; but he could not help admitting that he was still, as the looking-glass showed him, a very distinguished-looking man.

'Poor Sissy Miller!' he said, half laughing. How he would have liked to share that joke with his wife! He turned instinctively to her diary. 'Gilbert,' he read, opening it at random, 'looked so wonderful . . .' It was as if she had answered his question. Of course, she seemed to say, you're very attractive to women. Of course Sissy Miller felt that too. He read on. 'How proud I am to be his wife!' And he had always been very proud to be her husband. How often, when they dined out somewhere, he had looked at her across the table and said to himself, She is the loveliest woman here! He read on. That first year he had been standing for Parliament. They had toured his constituency. 'When Gilbert sat down the applause was terrific. The whole audience rose and sang: "For he's a jolly good fellow." I was quite overcome.' He remembered that, too. She had been sitting on the platform beside him. He could still see the glance she cast at him, and how she had tears in her eyes. And then? He turned the pages. They had gone to Venice. He recalled that happy holiday after the election. 'We had ices at Florians.' He smiled – she was still such a child; she loved ices. 'Gilbert gave me a most interesting account of the history of Venice. He told me that the

Doges* . . .' She had written it all out in her schoolgirl hand. One of the delights of travelling with Angela had been that she was so eager to learn. She was so terribly ignorant, she used to say, as if that were not one of her charms. And then – he opened the next volume – they had come back to London. 'I was so anxious to make a good impression. I wore my wedding dress.' He could see her now sitting next to old Sir Edward; and making a conquest of that formidable old man, his chief. He read on rapidly, filling in scene after scene from her scrappy fragments. 'Dined at the House of Commons* . . . To an evening party at the Lovegroves. Did I realize my responsibility, Lady L. asked me, as Gilbert's wife?' Then, as the years passed – he took another volume from the writing table – he had become more and more absorbed in his work. And she, of course, was more often alone . . . It had been a great grief to her, apparently, that they had had no children. 'How I wish,' one entry read, 'that Gilbert had a son!' Oddly enough he had never much regretted that himself. Life had been so full, so rich as it was. That year he had been given a minor post in the government. A minor post only, but her comment was: 'I am quite certain now that he will be Prime Minister!' Well, if things had gone differently, it might have been so. He paused here to speculate upon what might have been. Politics was a gamble, he reflected; but the game wasn't over yet. Not at fifty. He cast his eyes rapidly over more pages, full of the little trifles, the insignificant, happy daily trifles that had made up her life.

He took up another volume and opened it at random. 'What a coward I am! I let the chance slip again. But it seemed selfish to bother him with my own affairs, when he has so much to think about. And we so seldom have an evening alone.' What was the meaning of that? Oh, here was the explanation – it referred to her work in the East End*. 'I plucked up courage and talked to Gilbert at last. He was so kind, so good. He made no objection.' He remembered that conversation. She had told him that she felt so idle, so useless. She wished to have some work of her own. She wanted to do something – she had blushed so prettily, he remembered, as she said it, sitting in that very chair – to help others. He had bantered her a little. Hadn't she enough to do looking after him, after her home? Still, if it amused her, of course he had no objection. What was it? Some district? Some committee? Only she must promise not to make herself ill. So it seemed that every Wednesday she went to Whitechapel*. He remembered how he hated the clothes she wore on those occasions. But she had taken it very seriously, it seemed. The diary was full of references like this: 'Saw Mrs Jones . . . She has ten children . . . Husband lost his arm in an accident . . . Did my best to find a job for Lily.' He skipped on. His own name occurred less frequently. His interest slackened. Some of the entries conveyed nothing to him. For example: 'Had a heated argument about socialism with B. M.' Who was B. M.? he could not fill in the initials; some woman, he supposed, that she had met on one of her committees. 'B. M. made a violent attack upon the upper classes . . . I walked back after the meeting with B. M. and tried to convince him. But he is so narrow-minded.' So B. M. was a man – no doubt one of those 'intellectuals', as they call themselves, who are so violent, as Angela said, and so narrow-minded. She had invited him to come and see her apparently. 'B. M. came to dinner. He shook hands with Minnie!' That note of exclamation gave another twist to his mental picture. B. M., it seemed, wasn't used to parlourmaids; he had shaken hands with Minnie. Presumably he was one of those tame working men who air their views in ladies' drawing-rooms. Gilbert knew the type, and had no liking for this particular specimen, whoever B. M. might be. Here he was again. 'Went with B. M. to the Tower of London . . . He said revolution is bound to come . . . He said we live in a Fool's Paradise.' That was just the kind of thing B. M. would say – Gilbert could hear him. He could also see him quite distinctly – a stubby little man, with a rough beard, red tie, dressed as they always did in tweeds, who had never done an honest day's work in his life. Surely Angela had the sense to see through him? He read on. 'B. M. said some very disagreeable things about—.' The name was carefully scratched out. 'I told him I would not listen to any more abuse of —.' Again the name was obliterated. Could it have been his own name? Was that why Angela covered the page so quickly when he came in? The thought added to his growing dislike of B. M. He had had the impertinence to discuss him in this very room. Why had Angela never told him? It was very unlike her to conceal anything; she had been the soul of candour. He turned the pages, picking out every reference to B. M. 'B. M. told me the story of his childhood. His mother went out charring* . . . When I think of it, I can hardly bear to go on living in such luxury . . . Three guineas for one hat!' If only she had discussed the matter with him, instead of puzzling her poor little head about questions that were much too difficult for her to understand! He had lent her books. *Karl Marx**, *The Coming Revolution*. The initials B. M., B. M., B. M., recurred repeatedly. But why never the full name? There was an informality, an intimacy in the use of initials that was very unlike Angela. Had she called him B. M. to his face? He read on. 'B. M. came unexpectedly after dinner. Luckily, I was alone.' That was only a year ago. 'Luckily' – why luckily? – 'I was alone.' Where had he been that night? He checked the date in his engagement book. It had been the night of the Mansion House* dinner. And B. M. and Angela had spent the evening alone! He tried to recall that evening. Was she waiting up for him when he came back? Had the room looked just as usual? Were there glasses on the table? Were the chairs drawn close together? He could remember nothing – nothing whatever, nothing except his own speech at the Mansion House dinner. It became more and more inexplicable to him – the whole situation;

his wife receiving an unknown man alone. Perhaps the next volume would explain. Hastily he reached for the last of the diaries – the one she had left unfinished when she died. There, on the very first page, was that cursed fellow again. 'Dined alone with B. M. . . . He became very agitated. He said it was time we understood each other . . . I tried to make him listen. But he would not. He threatened that if I did not . . .' the rest of the page was scored over. She had written 'Egypt. Egypt. Egypt,' over the whole page. He could not make out a single word; but there could be only one interpretation: the scoundrel had asked her to become his mistress. Alone in his room! The blood rushed to Gilbert Clandon's face. He turned the pages rapidly. What had been her answer? Initials had ceased. It was simply 'he' now. 'He came again. I told him I could not come to any decision . . . I implored him to leave.' He had forced himself upon her in this very house. But why hadn't she told him? How could she have hesitated for an instant? Then: 'I wrote him a letter.' Then pages were left blank. Then there was this: 'No answer to my letter.' Then more blank pages; and then this: 'He has done what he threatened.' After that – what came after that? He turned page after page. All were blank. But there, on the very day before her death, was this entry: 'Have I the courage to do it too?' That was the end.

Gilbert Clandon let the book slide to the floor. He could see her in front of him. She was standing on the kerb in Piccadilly. Her eyes stared; her fists were clenched. Here came the car . . .

He could not bear it. He must know the truth. He strode to the telephone.

'Miss Miller!' There was silence. Then he heard someone moving in the room.

'Sissy Miller speaking' – her voice at last answered him.

'Who,' he thundered, 'is B. M.?'

He could hear the cheap clock ticking on her mantelpiece; then a long-drawn sigh. Then at last she said:

'He was my brother.'

He *was* her brother; her brother who had killed himself. 'Is there,' he heard Sissy Miller asking, 'anything that I can explain?'

'Nothing!' he cried. 'Nothing!'

He had received his legacy. She had told him the truth. She had stepped off the kerb to rejoin her lover. She had stepped off the kerb to escape from him.

NOTES

Piccadilly (p38)
a well-known shopping street in the centre of London
the Doges (p42)
the chief magistrates and rulers of the former republic of Venice
the House of Commons (p42)
the elected chamber of the UK Parliament
the East End, Whitechapel (p42, 43)
the part of London (Whitechapel is a district in the East End) where at
the time of this story mostly poor, working-class people lived
charring (p44)
(old-fashioned) working as a cleaner in someone else's house
Karl Marx (p44)
(1818–83) author of *Das Kapital* and the prophet of communism
Mansion House (p44)
the official residence of the Lord Mayor in the city of London

DISCUSSION

1 Angela could have destroyed her diaries, and Gilbert would never have
known about B. M. What might Angela's motive have been in leaving
her diaries for Gilbert – revenge, honesty, an explanation? Do you think
she was right to make sure Gilbert learnt the truth? Why, or why not?

2 Gilbert wishes Angela had discussed social matters with him, instead
of 'puzzling her poor little head about questions that were much too
difficult for her to understand'. What does this tell us about Gilbert?
Can you find other phrases that reinforce this impression of him?

3 Angela apparently refused to leave Gilbert and to go and live with B. M.
What might her reasons have been – a reluctance to hurt Gilbert, fear
of the social consequences, or something else? If she had gone to live
with B. M., do you think it would have been a happy, lasting
relationship? Explain the reasons for your view.

4 What do we learn about B. M.? Gilbert interprets B. M.'s shaking hands
with the parlourmaid as evidence that he was completely unused to
households with servants, but as B. M. was a fervent socialist, the
shaking of a servant's hand could have quite a different interpretation.
What might that be? And how would you describe each man's attitudes
towards politics and social class?

LANGUAGE FOCUS

1 When Sissy Miller came to collect her legacy, Gilbert had prepared a little speech, and Sissy replied as though she too had prepared a speech. Using formal language, write down what the two of them might have said when presenting and receiving the pearl brooch.

2 *'How I wish,' one entry read, 'that Gilbert had a son!' Oddly enough he had never much regretted that himself. Life had been so full, so rich as it was.*
   'Oddly enough' – why 'oddly'? And what effect is created by the absence of any determiner (e.g. 'his' or 'their') on the noun 'Life'?

3 Angela's diary finishes in a very fragmentary way, yet we understand everything that is implied; for example, what the 'it' in the last sentence below refers to. Try adding explanatory details and context to these sentences and phrases from the diary to make a continuous paragraph. Which version, yours or the one in the story, is more effective? Why?

   • *I tried to make him listen. But he would not. He threatened that if I did not . . . .*
   • *He came again. I told him I could not come to any decision . . . I implored him to leave.*
   • *I wrote him a letter.*
   • *No answer to my letter.*
   • *He has done what he threatened.*
   • *Have I the courage to do it too?*

ACTIVITIES

1 Was Gilbert a bad husband? How do you think the other characters saw him? Write three short descriptions of Gilbert, as seen by
   a) his wife Angela
   b) Sissy Miller
   c) Sissy Miller's brother, B.M.

2 Sissy Miller seems to feel sympathy for all three people in this tragic love triangle. Imagine that you are Sissy, and that Gilbert has changed his mind and asked you to 'explain'. Write him a letter, which is sympathetic to his feelings, but which also shows great understanding of the dilemma that Angela and her brother found themselves in.

A Painful Case

The Author

James Joyce was born in Dublin in 1882, and was educated at Jesuit schools and University College, Dublin. In 1902 he spent a year in Paris, living in poverty and writing poetry. After his mother's death, he returned to Europe with Nora Barnacle, with whom he spent the rest of his life and who bore him a son and a daughter. Early publications included *Chamber Music*, a book of verse, *Dubliners*, a volume of short stories, and *A Portrait of the Artist as a Young Man*, a largely autobiographical work. He received help and support from fellow writers, W. B. Yeats and Ezra Pound, but continued to struggle against poverty and problems with his eyes. His two greatest works, *Ulysses* (1922) and *Finnegans Wake* (1939), revolutionized the form of the novel and pushed linguistic experiment to the extreme limits of communication. He died in Zurich in 1941.

The Story

Emotions are hard to regulate; they can be disruptive, unsettling, but life would be rather bleak if ruled by cold reason alone. Even the pain of love should be welcomed, according to the poet Tennyson, who wrote:

'Tis better to have loved and lost

Than never to have loved at all.

But is that always true? It might seem hollow comfort if the loss of love and hope leads to unbearable loneliness.

At present love has no place in Mr James Duffy's life. He is an austere man, whose life follows an unrelenting pattern: a routine job in a Dublin bank and a domestic life of sombre regularity. The only departure from this ordered existence is an occasional visit to a concert, where one night a cautious conversation begins . . .

A PAINFUL CASE

M r James Duffy lived in Chapelizod because he wished to live
as far as possible from the city of which he was a citizen and
because he found all the other suburbs of Dublin mean, modern
and pretentious. He lived in an old sombre house and from his
windows he could look into the disused distillery or upwards along
the shallow river on which Dublin is built. The lofty walls of his
uncarpeted room were free from pictures. He had himself bought
every article of furniture in the room: a black iron bedstead, an iron
washstand, four cane chairs, a clothes-rack, a coal-scuttle, a fender
and irons and a square table on which lay a double desk. A bookcase
had been made in an alcove by means of shelves of white wood.
The bed was clothed with white bed-clothes and a black and scarlet
rug covered the foot. A little hand-mirror hung above the washstand
and during the day a white-shaded lamp stood as the sole ornament
of the mantelpiece. The books on the white wooden shelves were
arranged from below upwards according to bulk. A complete
Wordsworth* stood at one end of the lowest shelf and a copy of
the *Maynooth Catechism**, sewn into the cloth cover of a
notebook, stood at one end of the top shelf. Writing materials were
always on the desk. In the desk lay a manuscript translation of
Hauptmann's *Michael Kramer,* the stage directions of which were
written in purple ink, and a little sheaf of papers held together by
a brass pin. In these sheets a sentence was inscribed from time to
time and, in an ironical moment, the headline of an advertisement
for *Bile Beans** had been pasted on to the first sheet. On lifting the
lid of the desk a faint fragrance escaped – the fragrance of new
cedarwood pencils or of a bottle of gum or of an over-ripe apple
which might have been left there and forgotten.

Mr Duffy abhorred anything which betokened physical or mental disorder. A medieval doctor would have called him saturnine. His face, which carried the entire tale of his years, was of the brown tint of Dublin streets. On his long and rather large head grew dry black hair and a tawny moustache did not quite cover an unamiable mouth. His cheekbones also gave his face a harsh character; but there was no harshness in the eyes which, looking at the world from under their tawny eyebrows, gave the impression of a man ever alert to greet a redeeming instinct in others but often disappointed. He lived at a little distance from his body, regarding his own acts with doubtful side-glances. He had an odd autobiographical habit which led him to compose in his mind from time to time a short sentence about himself containing a subject in the third person and a predicate in the past tense. He never gave alms to beggars and walked firmly, carrying a stout hazel*.

He had been for many years cashier of a private bank in Baggot Street. Every morning he came in from Chapelizod by tram. At midday he went to Dan Burke's and took his lunch – a bottle of lager beer and a small trayful of arrowroot biscuits. At four o'clock he was set free. He dined in an eating-house in George's Street where he felt himself safe from the society of Dublin's gilded youth* and where there was a certain plain honesty in the bill of fare. His evenings were spent either before his landlady's piano or roaming about the outskirts of the city. His liking for Mozart's music brought him sometimes to an opera or a concert: these were the only dissipations of his life.

He had neither companions nor friends, church nor creed. He lived his spiritual life without any communion with others, visiting his relatives at Christmas and escorting them to the cemetery when they died. He performed these two social duties for old dignity's sake but conceded nothing further to the conventions which regulate the civic life. He allowed himself to think that in certain circumstances he would rob his bank but, as these circumstances never arose, his life rolled out evenly – an adventureless tale.

One evening he found himself sitting beside two ladies in the Rotunda. The house, thinly peopled and silent, gave distressing prophecy of failure. The lady who sat next him looked round at the deserted house once or twice and then said:

– What a pity there is such a poor house tonight! It's so hard on people to have to sing to empty benches.

He took the remark as an invitation to talk. He was surprised that she seemed so little awkward. While they talked he tried to fix her permanently in his memory. When he learned that the young girl beside her was her daughter he judged her to be a year or so younger than himself. Her face, which must have been handsome, had remained intelligent. It was an oval face with strongly marked features. The eyes were very dark blue and steady. Their gaze began with a defiant note, but was confused by what seemed a deliberate swoon of the pupil into the iris, revealing for an instant a temperament of great sensibility. The pupil reasserted itself quickly, this half-disclosed nature fell again under the reign of prudence, and her astrakhan jacket, moulding a bosom of a certain fullness, struck the note of defiance more definitely.

He met her again a few weeks afterwards at a concert in Earlsfort Terrace and seized the moments when her daughter's attention was diverted to become intimate. She alluded once or twice to her husband but her tone was not such as to make the allusion a warning. Her name was Mrs Sinico. Her husband's great-great-grandfather had come from Leghorn. Her husband was captain of a mercantile boat plying between Dublin and Holland; and they had one child.

Meeting her a third time by accident he found courage to make an appointment. She came. This was the first of many meetings; they met always in the evening and chose the most quiet quarters for their walks together. Mr Duffy, however, had a distaste for underhand ways and, finding that they were compelled to meet stealthily, he forced her to ask him to her house. Captain Sinico encouraged his visits, thinking that his daughter's hand was in question. He had dismissed his wife so sincerely from his gallery of pleasures that he did not suspect that anyone else would take an interest in her. As the husband was often away and the daughter out giving music lessons Mr Duffy had many opportunities of enjoying the lady's society. Neither he nor she had had any such adventure before and neither was conscious of any incongruity. Little by little he entangled his thoughts with hers. He lent her books, provided her with ideas, shared his intellectual life with her. She listened to all.

Sometimes in return for his theories she gave out some fact of her own life. With almost maternal solicitude she urged him to let his nature open to the full; she became his confessor. He told her that for some time he had assisted at the meetings of an Irish Socialist Party where he had felt himself a unique figure amidst a score of sober workmen in a garret lit by an inefficient oil-lamp. When the party had divided into three sections, each under its own leader and in its own garret, he had discontinued his attendances. The workmen's discussions, he said, were too timorous; the interest they took in the question of wages was inordinate. He felt that they were hard-featured realists and that they resented an exactitude which was the product of a leisure not within their reach. No social revolution, he told her, would be likely to strike Dublin for some centuries.

She asked him why did he not write out his thoughts. For what, he asked her, with careful scorn. To compete with phrasemongers, incapable of thinking consecutively for sixty seconds? To submit himself to the criticisms of an obtuse middle class which entrusted its morality to policemen and its fine arts to impresarios?

He went often to her little cottage outside Dublin; often they spent their evenings alone. Little by little, as their thoughts entangled, they spoke of subjects less remote. Her companionship was like a warm soil about an exotic. Many times she allowed the dark to fall upon them, refraining from lighting the lamp. The dark discreet room, their isolation, the music that still vibrated in their ears united them. This union exalted him, wore away the rough edges of his character, emotionalized his mental life. Sometimes he caught himself listening to the sound of his own voice. He thought that in her eyes he would ascend to an angelical stature; and, as he attached the fervent nature of his companion more and more closely to him, he heard the strange impersonal voice which he recognized as his own, insisting on the soul's incurable loneliness. We cannot give ourselves, it said: we are our own. The end of these discourses was that one night, during which she had shown every sign of unusual excitement, Mrs Sinico caught up his hand passionately and pressed it to her cheek.

Mr Duffy was very much surprised. Her interpretation of his words disillusioned him. He did not visit her for a week; then he wrote to her asking her to meet him. As he did not wish their last interview to be troubled by the influence of their ruined confessional they met in a little cakeshop near the Parkgate. It was cold autumn weather but in spite of the cold they wandered up and down the roads of the Park for nearly three hours. They agreed to break off their intercourse: every bond, he said, is a bond to sorrow. When they came out of the Park they walked in silence towards the tram; but here she began to tremble so violently that, fearing another collapse on her part, he bade her goodbye quickly and left her. A few days later he received a parcel containing his books and music.

Four years passed. Mr Duffy returned to his even way of life. His room still bore witness of the orderliness of his mind. Some new pieces of music encumbered the music-stand in the lower room and on his shelves stood two volumes by Nietzsche*: *Thus Spake Zarathustra* and *The Gay Science*. He wrote seldom in the sheaf of papers which lay in his desk. One of his sentences, written two months after his last interview with Mrs Sinico, read: Love between man and man is impossible because there must not be sexual intercourse and friendship between man and woman is impossible because there must be sexual intercourse. He kept away from concerts lest he should meet her. His father died; the junior partner of the bank retired. And still every morning he went into the city by tram and every evening walked home from the city after having dined moderately in George's Street and read the evening paper for dessert.

One evening as he was about to put a morsel of corned beef and cabbage into his mouth his hand stopped. His eyes fixed themselves on a paragraph in the evening paper which he had propped against the water-carafe. He replaced the morsel of food on his plate and read the paragraph attentively. Then he drank a glass of water, pushed his plate to one side, doubled the paper down before him between his elbows and read the paragraph over and over again. The cabbage began to deposit a cold white grease on his plate. The girl came over to him to ask was his dinner not properly cooked. He said it was very good and ate a few mouthfuls of it with difficulty. Then he paid his bill and went out.

He walked along quickly through the November twilight, his stout hazel stick striking the ground regularly, the fringe of the buff *Mail* peeping out of a side-pocket of his tight reefer overcoat. On the lonely road which leads from the Parkgate to Chapelizod he slackened his pace. His stick struck the ground less emphatically and his breath, issuing irregularly, almost with a sighing sound, condensed in the wintry air. When he reached his house he went up at once to his bedroom and, taking the paper from his pocket, read the paragraph again by the failing light of the window. He read it not aloud, but moving his lips as a priest does when he reads the prayers *Secreto*. This was the paragraph:

DEATH OF A LADY AT SYDNEY PARADE
A PAINFUL CASE

Today at the City of Dublin Hospital the Deputy Coroner (in the absence of Mr Leverett) held an inquest on the body of Mrs Emily Sinico, aged forty-three years, who was killed at Sydney Parade Station yesterday evening. The evidence showed that the deceased lady, while attempting to cross the line, was knocked down by the engine of the ten o'clock slow train from Kingstown, thereby sustaining injuries of the head and right side which led to her death.

James Lennon, driver of the engine, stated that he had been in the employment of the railway company for fifteen years. On hearing the guard's whistle he set the train in motion and a second or two afterwards brought it to rest in response to loud cries. The train was going slowly.

P. Dunne, railway porter, stated that as the train was about to start he observed a woman attempting to cross the lines. He ran towards her and shouted but, before he could reach her, she was caught by the buffer of the engine and fell to the ground.

A juror—You saw the lady fall?

Witness—Yes.

Police Sergeant Croly deposed that when he arrived he found the deceased lying on the platform apparently dead. He had the body taken to the waiting-room pending the arrival of the ambulance.

Constable 57E corroborated.

Dr Halpin, assistant house-surgeon of the City of Dublin Hospital, stated that the deceased had two lower ribs fractured and had sustained severe contusions of the right shoulder. The right side of the head had been injured in the fall. The injuries were not sufficient to have caused death in a normal person. Death, in his opinion, had been probably due to shock and sudden failure of the heart's action.

Mr H. B. Patterson Finlay, on behalf of the railway company, expressed his deep regret at the accident. The company had always taken every precaution to prevent people crossing the lines except by the bridges, both by placing notices in every station and by the use of patent spring gates at level crossings. The deceased had been in the habit of crossing the lines late at night from platform to platform and, in view of certain other circumstances of the case, he did not think the railway officials were to blame.

Captain Sinico, of Leoville, Sydney Parade, husband of the deceased, also gave evidence. He stated that the deceased was his wife. He was not in Dublin at the time of the accident as he had arrived only that morning from Rotterdam. They had been married for twenty-two years and had lived happily until about two years ago when his wife began to be rather intemperate in her habits.

Miss Mary Sinico said that of late her mother had been in the habit of going out at night to buy spirits. She, witness, had often tried to reason with her mother and had induced her to join a League*. She was not at home until an hour after the accident.

The jury returned a verdict in accordance with the medical evidence and exonerated Lennon from all blame.

The Deputy Coroner said it was a most painful case, and expressed great sympathy with Captain Sinico and his daughter. He urged on the railway company to take strong measures to prevent the possibility of similar accidents in the future. No blame attached to anyone.

* * *

Mr Duffy raised his eyes from the paper and gazed out of his window on the cheerless evening landscape. The river lay quiet beside the empty distillery and from time to time a light appeared in some house on the Lucan road. What an end! The whole narrative of her death revolted him and it revolted him to think that he had ever spoken to her of what he held sacred. The threadbare phrases, the inane expressions of sympathy, the cautious words of a reporter won over to conceal the details of commonplace vulgar death attacked his stomach. Not merely had she degraded herself; she had degraded him. He saw the squalid tract of her vice, miserable and malodorous. His soul's companion! He thought of the hobbling wretches whom he had seen carrying cans and bottles to be filled by the barman. Just God, what an end! Evidently she had been unfit to live, without any strength of purpose, an easy prey to habits, one of the wrecks on which civilisation has been reared. But that she could have sunk so low! Was it possible he had deceived himself so utterly about her? He remembered her outburst of that night and interpreted it in a harsher sense than he had ever done. He had no difficulty now in approving of the course he had taken.

As the light failed and his memory began to wander he thought her hand touched his. The shock which had first attacked his stomach was now attacking his nerves. He put on his overcoat and hat quickly and went out. The cold air met him on the threshold; it crept into the sleeves of his coat. When he came to the public-house at Chapelizod Bridge he went in and ordered a hot punch.

The proprietor served him obsequiously but did not venture to talk. There were five or six working-men in the shop discussing the value of a gentleman's estate in County Kildare. They drank at intervals from their huge pint tumblers and smoked, spitting often on the floor and sometimes dragging the sawdust over their spits with their heavy boots. Mr Duffy sat on his stool and gazed at them, without seeing or hearing them. After a while they went out and he called for another punch. He sat a long time over it. The shop was very quiet. The proprietor sprawled on the counter reading the *Herald* and yawning. Now and again a tram was heard swishing along the lonely road outside.

As he sat there, living over his life with her and evoking alternately the two images in which he now conceived her, he realized that she was dead, that she had ceased to exist, that she had become a memory. He began to feel ill at ease. He asked himself what else could he have done. He could not have carried on a comedy of deception with her; he could not have lived with her openly. He had done what seemed to him best. How was he to blame? Now that she was gone he understood how lonely her life must have been, sitting night after night, alone in that room. His life would be lonely too until he, too, died, ceased to exist, became a memory – if anyone remembered him.

It was after nine o'clock when he left the shop. The night was cold and gloomy. He entered the park by the first gate and walked along under the gaunt trees. He walked through the bleak alleys where they had walked four years before. She seemed to be near him in the darkness. At moments he seemed to feel her voice touch his ear, her hand touch his. He stood still to listen. Why had he withheld life from her? Why had he sentenced her to death? He felt his moral nature falling to pieces.

When he gained the crest of the Magazine Hill he halted and looked along the river towards Dublin, the lights of which burned redly and hospitably in the cold night. He looked down the slope and, at the base, in the shadow of the wall of the park, he saw some human figures lying. Those venal and furtive loves filled him with despair. He gnawed the rectitude of his life; he felt that he had been outcast from life's feast. One human being had seemed to love him and he had denied her life and happiness: he had sentenced her to ignominy, a death of shame. He knew that the prostrate creatures down by the wall were watching him and wished him gone. No one wanted him; he was outcast from life's feast. He turned his eyes to the grey gleaming river, winding along towards Dublin. Beyond the river he saw a goods train winding out of Kingsbridge Station, like a worm with a fiery head winding through the darkness, obstinately and laboriously. It passed slowly out of sight; but still he heard in his ears the laborious drone of the engine reiterating the syllables of her name.

He turned back the way he had come, the rhythm of the engine pounding in his ears. He began to doubt the reality of what memory told him. He halted under a tree and allowed the rhythm to die away. He could not feel her near him in the darkness nor her voice touch his ear. He waited for some minutes listening. He could hear nothing: the night was perfectly silent. He listened again: perfectly silent. He felt that he was alone.

NOTES

a complete Wordsworth (p50)

the collected poems of William Wordsworth (1770–1850), a famous English poet

Maynooth Catechism (p50)

a summary of the principles of the Roman Catholic religion in the form of questions and answers (Maynooth is a village near Dublin, with a famous training college for Roman Catholic priests)

Bile Beans (p50)

these were 'liver' pills, to soothe an upset digestive system; 'bile' can mean both a liquid produced by the liver, and anger or hatred

a stout hazel (p51)

a walking stick cut from a hazel tree

gilded youth (p51)

(literary) rich, upper-class young people

Nietzsche (p55)

a German philosopher (1844–1900); his writings were anti-Christianity and proposed a theory of a dominant 'master-class' in the human race

a League (p57)

a temperance league; an organization whose members promise to abstain from alcoholic drink

DISCUSSION

1 How would you describe Mr James Duffy and his attitudes towards his fellow human beings – his relatives, the workmen in the Irish Socialist Party, and Mrs Sinico?

2 The story is told from Mr Duffy's point of view and we see Mrs Sinico only through his eyes. Because of that, do you feel that Mrs Sinico is a shadowy presence? If so, do you think that makes the story less effective? Why, or why not? What, if anything, do we learn about her personality and character?

3 Mr Duffy was displeased and disillusioned when Mrs Sinico showed that she was emotionally involved. Why did he bring the relationship to an abrupt halt? Do you think he was right to do so? Why, or why not? What might have happened if their relationship had continued?

LANGUAGE FOCUS

1 This story is told in formal, rather literary language. Look again at the sentences and phrases below, and reformulate them in less literary, more colloquial language.

- *Mr Duffy abhorred anything which betokened physical or mental disorder.* (p50)
- *The house, thinly peopled and silent, gave distressing prophecy of failure.* (p52)
- *. . . thinking that his daughter's hand was in question.* (p53)
- *He had dismissed his wife so sincerely from his gallery of pleasures . . .* (p53)
- *He felt his moral nature falling to pieces.* (p59)
- *. . . he felt that he had been outcast from life's feast.* (p59)

2 The 'cautious words' of the newspaper report of Mrs Sinico's death avoid explicit details, although Mr Duffy has no difficulty in reading between the lines. How might the following phrases be expressed in a modern, much more explicit style of reporting?

- *. . . in view of certain other circumstances of the case, he did not think the railway officials were to blame.*
- *. . . when his wife began to be rather intemperate in her habits.*
- *The jury returned a verdict in accordance with the medical evidence*
- *. . . to prevent the possibility of similar accidents in the future.*

ACTIVITIES

1 How do you think Mrs Sinico viewed Mr Duffy? Imagine that she kept a diary and write two short entries for it: one for the day of her third chance meeting with Mr Duffy, when he 'found courage to make an appointment' with her; and one for the day of their final meeting when they 'agreed to break off their intercourse'.

2 How did you interpret the ending of the story? As Mr Duffy walked through the park, he 'felt his moral nature falling to pieces'. Do you think that this sense of guilt was a feeling that would never leave him? Or was it temporary, and that by the time he 'felt that he was alone' he had already begun to dismiss the memory of Mrs Sinico from his mind? Write one more paragraph, as a postscript to the story, describing James Duffy's emotional state during the next year or two.

THE KIMONO

THE AUTHOR

Herbert Ernest Bates was born in England in 1905. He wrote his first novel, *The Two Sisters* (1926), while working in the office of a shoe factory warehouse. In World War II he joined the Royal Air Force, and as well as his wartime duties, was employed as the Armed Forces' first short-story writer, writing under the name of 'Flying Officer X'. During this time he published many short stories and his most famous novel, *Fair Stood the Wind for France* (1944). Another novel, *The Jacaranda Tree* (1949), was based on his wartime experiences in Burma. Many of his novels have been successfully televised, including *The Darling Buds of May* (1958), the first of his very popular stories about the Larkin family, which show his deep love of the English countryside and the beauty of nature. He died in 1974.

THE STORY

A chance encounter can change the course of a life in an instant. Whether for the worse or the better is often not apparent until some time later. Looking back, we wonder how that meeting came about, what events – insignificant in themselves – combined to change our destiny. Was it the state of the weather that day, the choice of a woman's dress, a moment's indecision?

When Arthur Lawson emerges from his job interview into the fierce sunshine of the London streets, he feels very content. A good job awaits him, he is engaged to a nice girl from a respectable family, his future life is neatly mapped out before him. But then he gets lost trying to find his hotel, and the heat on this August day is terrific, almost tropical. He just has to get out of the sun for a moment and find something cool to drink . . .

THE KIMONO

It was the second Saturday of August, 1911, when I came to London for the interview with Kersch and Co. I was just twenty-five. The summer had been almost tropical.

There used to be a train in those days that got into St Pancras, from the North, about ten in the morning. I came by it from Nottingham, left my bag in the cloakroom and went straight down to the City by bus. The heat of London was terrific, a white dust heat, thick with horse dung. I had put on my best suit, a blue serge, and it was like a suit of gauze. The heat seemed to stab at me through it.

Kersch and Co. were very nice. They were electrical engineers. I had applied for a vacancy advertised by them. That morning I was on the short list and Mr Alexander Kersch, the son, was very nice to me. We talked a good deal about Nottingham and I asked him if he knew the Brownsons, who were prominent Congregationalists* there, but he said no. Everyone in Nottingham, almost, knew the Brownsons, but I suppose it did not occur to me in my excitement that Kersch was a Jew. After a time he offered me a whisky and soda, but I refused. I had been brought up rather strictly, and in any case the Brownsons would not have liked it. Finally, Mr Kersch asked me if I could be in London over the weekend. I said yes, and he asked me at once to come in on Monday morning. I knew then that the job was as good as settled and I was trembling with excitement as I shook hands and said goodbye.

I came out of Kersch and Co. just before twelve o'clock. Their offices were somewhere off Cheapside. I forget the name of the street. I only remember, now, how very hot it was. There was something un-English about it. It was a terrific heat, fierce and white. And I made up my mind to go straight back to St Pancras and get my bag and take it to the hotel the Brownsons had recommended to me. It was so hot that I did not want to eat. I felt that if I could get my room and wash and rest it would be enough. I could eat later. I would go up West* and do myself rather well.

Pa Brownson had outlined the position of the hotel so well, both in conversation and on paper, that when I came out of St Pancras with my bag I felt I knew the way to the street as well as if it had been in Nottingham. I turned east and then north and went on turning left and then right, until finally I came to the place where the street with the hotel ought to have been. It wasn't there. I couldn't believe it. I walked about a bit, always coming back to the same place again in case I should get lost. Then I asked a baker's boy where Midhope Street was and he didn't know. I asked one or two more people, and they didn't know either. 'Wade's Hotel,' I would say, to make it clearer, but it was no good. Then a man said he thought I should go back towards St Pancras a bit, and ask again, and I did.

It must have been about two o'clock when I knew that I was pretty well lost. The heat was shattering. I saw one or two other hotels, but they looked a bit low class and I was tired and desperate.

Finally I set my bag down in the shade and wiped my face. The sweat on me was filthy. I was wretched. The Brownsons had been so definite about the hotel and I knew that when I got back they would ask me if I liked it and all about it. Hilda would want to know about it too. Later on, if I got the Kersch job, we should be coming up to it for our honeymoon.

At last I picked up my bag again. Across the street was a little sweet shop and café, showing ices. I went across to it. I felt I had to have something.

In the shop a big woman with black hair was tinkering with the ice-cream mixer. Something had gone wrong. I saw that at once. It was just my luck.

'I suppose it's no use asking for an ice?' I said.

'Well, if you wouldn't mind *waiting*.'

'How long?'

'As soon as ever I get this nut fixed on and the freezer going again. We've had a breakdown.'

'All right. You don't mind if I sit down?' I said.

She said no, and I sat down and leaned one elbow on the tea-table, the only one there was. The woman went on tinkering with the freezer. She was a heavy woman, about fifty, a little swarthy, and rather masterful to look at. The shop was stifling and filled with a sort of yellowish-pink shade cast by the sun pouring through the shop blind.

'I suppose it's no use asking you where Midhope Street is?' I said.

'Midhope Street,' she said. She put her tongue in her cheek, in thought. 'Midhope Street, I ought to know that.'

'Or Wade's Hotel.'

'Wade's Hotel,' she said. She wriggled her tongue between her teeth. They were handsome teeth, very white. 'Wade's Hotel. No. That beats me.' And then: 'Perhaps my daughter will know. I'll call her.'

She straightened up to call into the back of the shop. But a second before she opened her mouth the girl herself came in. She looked surprised to see me there.

'Oh, here you are, Blanche! This gentlemen here is looking for Wade's Hotel.'

'I'm afraid I'm lost,' I said.

'Wade's Hotel,' the girl said. She too stood in thought, running her tongue over her teeth, and her teeth too were very white, like her mother's. 'Wade's Hotel. I've seen that somewhere. Surely?'

'Midhope Street,' I said.

'Midhope Street.'

No, she couldn't remember. She had on a sort of kimono, loose, with big orange flowers all over it. I remember thinking it was rather fast*. For those days it was. It wouldn't be now. And somehow, because it was so loose and brilliant, I couldn't take my eyes off it. It made me uneasy, but it was an uneasiness in which there was pleasure as well, almost excitement. I remember thinking she was really half undressed. The kimono had no neck and no sleeves. It was simply a piece of material that wrapped over her, and when suddenly she bent down and tried to fit the last screw on to the freezer the whole kimono fell loose and I could see her body.

At the same time something else happened. Her hair fell over her shoulder. It was the time of very long hair, the days when girls would pride themselves that they could sit on their pig-tails, but hers was the longest hair I had ever seen. It was like the thick jet-black cotton-rope. And when she bent down over the freezer the pig-tail of it was so long that the tip touched the ice.

'I'm so sorry,' the girl said. 'My hair's always getting me into trouble.'

'It's all right. It just seems to be my unlucky day, that's all.'

'I'm so sorry.'

'Will you have a cup of tea?' the woman said. 'Instead of the ice? Instead of waiting?'

'That's it, Mother. Get him some tea. You *would* like tea, wouldn't you?'

'Very much.'

So the woman went through the counter-flap into the back of the shop to get the tea. The girl and I, in the shop alone, stood and looked at the freezer. I felt queer in some way, uneasy. The girl had not troubled to tighten up her kimono. She let it hang loose, anyhow, so that all the time I could see part of her shoulder and now and then her breasts. Her skin was very white, and once when she leaned forward rather further than usual I could have sworn that she had nothing on at all underneath.

'You keep looking at my kimono,' she said. 'Do you like it?'

'It's very nice,' I said. 'It's very nice stuff.'

'Lovely stuff. Feel of it. Go on. Just feel of it.'

I felt the stuff. For some reason, perhaps it was because I had had no food, I felt weak. And she knew it. She must have known it. 'It's lovely stuff. Feel it. I made it myself.' She spoke sweetly and softly, in invitation. There was something electric about her. I listened quite mechanically. From the minute she asked me to feel the stuff of her kimono I was quite helpless. She had me, as it were, completely done up in the tangled maze of the orange and green of its flowers and leaves.

'Are you in London for long? Only today?'

'Until Monday.'

'I suppose you booked your room at the hotel?'

'No. I didn't book it. But I was strongly recommended there.'

'I see.'

That was all, only 'I see.' But in it there was something quite maddening. It was a kind of passionate veiled hint, a secret invitation.

'Things were going well,' I said, 'until I lost my way.'

'Oh!'

'I came up for an interview and I got the job. At least I think I got the job.'

'A bit of luck. I hope it's a good one?'

'Yes,' I said. 'It is. Kersch and Co. In the City.'

'Kersch and Co.?' she said. 'Not really? Kersch and Co.?'

'Yes,' I said. 'Why, do you know them?'

'Know them? Of course I know them. Everybody knows them. That *is* a bit of luck for you.'

And really I was flattered. She knew Kersch and Co.! She knew that it was a good thing. I think I was more pleased because of the attitude of the Brownsons. Kersch and Co. didn't mean anything to the Brownsons. It was just a name. They had been rather cold about it. I think they would have liked me to get the job, but they wouldn't have broken their hearts if I hadn't. Certainly they hadn't shown any excitement.

'Kersch and Co.,' the girl said again. 'That really *is* a bit of luck.'

Then the woman came in with the tea. 'Would you like anything to eat?'

'Well, I've had no dinner.'

'Oh! No wonder you look tired. I'll get you a sandwich. Is that all right?'

'Thank you.'

So the woman went out to get the sandwich, and the girl and I stayed in the shop again, alone.

'It's a pity you booked your room at the hotel,' she said.

'I haven't booked it,' I said.

'Oh! I thought you said you'd *booked* it. Oh! My fault. You *haven't* booked it?'

'No. Why?'

'We take people in here,' she said. 'Over the café. It's not central of course. But then we don't charge so much.'

I thought of the Brownsons. 'Perhaps I ought to go to the hotel,' I said.

'We charge three and six,' she said. 'That isn't much, is it?'

'Oh, no!'

'Why don't you just come up and see the room?' she said. 'Just come up.'

'Well . . .'

'Come up and see it. It won't eat you.'

She opened the rear door of the shop and in a moment I was going upstairs behind her. She was not wearing any stockings. Her bare legs were beautifully strong and white. The room was over the café. It was a very good room for three and six. The new wallpaper was silver-leaved and the bed was white and looked cool.

And suddenly it seemed silly to go out into the heat again and wander about looking for Wade's Hotel when I could stay where I was.

'Well, what do you think of it?' she said.

'I like it.'

She sat down on the bed. The kimono was drawn up over her legs and where it parted at her knees I could see her thighs, strong and white and softly disappearing into the shadow of the kimono. It was the day of long rather prim skirts and I had never seen a woman's legs like that. There was nothing between Hilda and me beyond kissing. All we had done was to talk of things, but there was nothing in it. Hilda always used to say that she would keep herself for me*.

The girl hugged her knees. I could have sworn she had nothing on under the kimono.

'I don't want to press you,' she said, 'but I do wish you'd stay. You'd be our first let.'

Suddenly a great wave of heat came up from the street outside, the fierce, horse-smelling, dust-white heat of the earlier day, and I said:

'All right. I'll stay.'

'Oh, you angel!'

The way she said that was so warm and frank that I did not know what to do. I simply smiled. I felt curiously weak with pleasure. Standing there, I could smell suddenly not only the heat but the warmth of her own body. It was sweetish and pungent, the soft odour of sweat and perfume. My heart was racing.

Then suddenly she got up and smoothed the kimono over her knees and thighs.

'My father has just died, you see,' she said. 'We are trying this for a living. You'll give us a start.'

Somehow it seemed too good to be true.

* * *

I know now that it was. But I will say more of that later, when the time comes.

That evening I came down into the shop again about six o'clock. I had had my tea and unpacked my things and rested. It was not much cooler, but I felt better. I was glad I had stayed.

The girl, Blanche, was sitting behind the counter, fanning herself with the broken lid of a sweet-box. She had taken off her kimono and was wearing a white gauzy dress with a black sash. I was disappointed. I think she must have seen that, because she pouted a bit when I looked at her. In turn I was glad she pouted. It made her lips look full-blooded and rich and shining. There was something lovely about her when she was sulky.

'Going out?' she said.

'Yes,' I said. 'I thought of going up West and celebrating over Kersch and Co.'

'Celebrating? By yourself?'

'Well,' I said. 'I'm alone. There's no one else.'

'Lucky you.'

I knew what she meant in a moment. 'Well,' I said, almost in a joke, 'why don't you come?'

'Me?' she said, eyes wide open. 'You don't mean it. Me?'

'I do,' I said. 'I do mean it.'

She got up. 'How long can you wait? I'll just change my dress and tell mother.'

'No hurry at all,' I said, and she ran upstairs.

I have said nothing about how old she was. In the kimono she looked about twenty, and in the white dress about the same age, perhaps a little younger. When she came down again that evening she looked nearer twenty-six or twenty-seven. She looked big and mature. She had changed from the white dress into a startling yellow affair with a sort of black coatee cut away at the hips. It was so flashy that I felt uneasy. It was very tight too: the skirt so tight that I could see every line of her body, the bodice filled tight in turn with her big breasts. I forgot what her hat was like. I rather fancy I thought it was rather silly. But later she took it off.

'Well, where shall we go?' she said.

'I thought of going up West and eating and perhaps dropping in to hear some music.'

'Music. Isn't that rather dull?'

'Well, a play then.'

'I say,' she said, 'don't let's go up West. Let's go down to the East End instead. We can have some fun. It'll do you good to see how the Jews live. If you're going to work for a firm of Jews you ought to know something about them. We might have some Jewish food. I know a nice place.'

So we took a bus and went. In the Mile End Road we had a meal. I didn't like it. The food didn't smell very nice. It was spiced and strong and rather strange to eat. But Blanche liked it. Finally she said she was thirsty. 'Let's go out of here and have a drink somewhere else,' she said. 'I know a place where you can get beautiful wine, cheap.' So we went from that restaurant to another. We had some cheese and a bottle of wine – asti, I think it was. The place was Italian. The evening was stifling and everywhere people were drinking heavily and fanning themselves limply against the heat. After the wine I began to feel rather strange. I wasn't used to it and I hardly knew what I was doing. The cheese was rather salty and made me thirsty. I kept drinking almost unconsciously and my lips began to form syllables roundly and loosely. I kept staring at Blanche and thinking of her in the kimono. She in turn would stare back and we played a kind of game, carrying on a kind of conversation with glances, burning each other up, until at last she said:

'What's your name? You haven't told me yet.'

'Arthur,' I said. 'Arthur Lawson.'

'Arthur.'

The way she said it set my heart on fire. I just couldn't say anything: I simply sat looking at her. There was an intimacy then, at that moment, in the mere silences and glances between us, that went far beyond anything I had known with Hilda.

Then she saw something on the back of the menu that made her give a little cry.

'Oh, there's a circus! Oh, let's go! Oh, Arthur, you must take me.'

So we went there too. I forget the name of the theatre and really, except for some little men and women with wizened bird faces and bears, there is nothing I remember except one thing. In the middle of the show was a trapeze act. A girl was swinging backwards and forwards across the stage in readiness to somersault and the drum was rolling to rouse the audience to excitement. Suddenly the girl shouted 'I can't do it!' and let loose. She crashed down into the stalls and in a minute half the audience were standing up in a pandemonium of terror.

'Oh! Arthur, take me out.'

We went out directly. In those days women fainted more often and more easily than they do now, and I thought Blanche would faint too. As we came out into the street she leaned against me heavily and clutched my arm.

'I'll get a cab and take you home,' I said.

'Something to drink first.'

I was a bit upset myself. We had a glass of port in a public house. It must have been about ten o'clock. Before long, after the rest and the port, Blanche's eyes were quite bright again.

Soon after that we took the cab and drove home. 'Let me lean against you,' she said. I took her and held her. 'That's it,' she said. 'Hold me. Hold me tight.' It was so hot in the cab that I could hardly breathe and I could feel her face hot and moist too. 'You're so hot,' I said. She said it was her dress. The velvet coatee was too warm. 'I'll change it as soon as I get home,' she said. 'Then we'll have a drink. Some ice-cream in lemonade. That'll be nice.'

In the cab I looked down at her hair. It was amazingly black. I smiled at it softly. It was full of odours that were warm and voluptuous. But it was the blackness of it that was so wonderful and so lovely.

'Why do they call you Blanche?' I said. 'When you're so black. Blanche means white.'

'How do you know I'm not white underneath?' she said.

I could not speak. No conversation I had ever had with a woman had ever gone within miles of that single sentence. I sat dead, my heart racing. I did not know what to do. 'Hold me tight,' she said. I held her and kissed her.

I got out of the cab mechanically. In the shop she went straight upstairs. I kept thinking of what she had said. I was wild with a new and for me a delicious excitement. Downstairs the shop was in darkness and finally I could not wait for her to come down again. I went quietly upstairs to meet her.

She was coming across the landing as I reached the head of the stairs. She was in the kimono, in her bare feet.

'Where are you?' she said softly. 'I can't see you.' She came a second later and touched me.

'Just let me see if mother has turned your bed back,' she whispered.

She went into my bedroom. I followed her. She was leaning over the bed. My heart was racing with a sensation of great longing for her. She smoothed the bed with her hands and, as she did so, the kimono, held no longer, fell right apart.

And as she turned again I could see, even in the darkness, that she had nothing on underneath it at all.

* * *

On the following Monday morning I saw Kersch and Co. again and in the afternoon I went back to Nottingham. I had been given the job.

But curiously, for a reason I could not explain, I was no longer excited. I kept thinking of Blanche. I suppose, what with my engagement to Hilda Brownson and so on, I ought to have been uneasy and a little conscience-stricken. I was uneasy, but it was a mad uneasiness and there was no conscience at all in it. I felt reckless and feverish, almost desperate. Blanche was the first woman I had known at all on terms of intimacy, and it shattered me. All my complacent values of love and women were smashed. I had slept with Blanche on Saturday night and again on Sunday and the effect on me was one of almost catastrophic ecstasy.

That was something I had never known at all with Hilda. I had never come near it. I am not telling this, emphasising the physical side of it and singling out the more passionate implications of it, merely for the sake of telling it. I want to make clear that I had undergone a revolution: a revolution brought about, too, simply by a kimono and a girl's bare body underneath it. And since it was a revolution that changed my whole life it seems to me that I ought to make the colossal effect of it quite clear, now and for always.

I know, now, that I ought to have broken it off with Hilda at once. But I didn't. She was so pleased at my getting the Kersch job that to have told her would have been as cruel as taking away a doll from a child. I couldn't tell her.

A month later we were married. My heart was simply not in it. I was not there. All the time I was thinking of and, in imagination, making love to Blanche. We spent our honeymoon at Bournemouth in September. Kersch and Co. had been very nice and the result was that I was not to take up the new appointment until the twenty-fifth of the month.

I say appointment. It was the word the Brownsons always used.

From the very first they were not very much in love with my going to work in London at all and taking Hilda with me. I myself had no parents, but Hilda was their only child. That put what seemed to me a snobbish premium on her. They set her on a pedestal. My job was nothing beside Hilda. They began to dictate what we should do and how and where we ought to live, and finally, Mrs Brownson suggested that we all go to London and choose the flat in which we were to live. I objected. Then Hilda cried and there was an unpleasant scene in which Pa Brownson said that he thought I was unreasonable and that all Mrs Brownson was trying to do was to ensure that I could give Hilda as good a home as she had always had. He said something else about God guiding us as He had always guided them. We must put our trust in God. But God or no God, I was determined that if we were going to live in a flat in London the Brownsons shouldn't choose it. I would choose it myself. Because even then I knew where, if it was humanly possible, I wanted it to be.

In the end I went to London by myself. I talked round Hilda, and Hilda talked round her mother, and her mother, I suppose, talked round her father. At any rate I went. We decided on a flat at twenty-five shillings a week if we could get it. It was then about the twentieth of September.

I went straight from St Pancras to Blanche. It was a lovely day, blue and soft. It was a pain for me merely to be alive. I got to the shop just as Blanche was going out. We almost bumped into each other.

'Arthur!'

The way she said it made me almost sick with joy. She had on a tight fawn costume and a little fussy brown hat. 'Arthur! I was just going out. You just caught me. But mother can go instead. Oh! Arthur.' Her mother came out of the back room and in a minute Blanche had taken off her hat and costume and her mother had gone out instead of her, leaving us alone in the shop.

We went straight upstairs. There was no decision, no asking, no consent in it at all. We went straight up out of a tremendous equal passion for each other. We were completely in unison, in desire and act and consummation and everything. Someone came in the shop and rang the bell loudly while we were upstairs, but it made no difference. We simply existed for each other. There was no outside world. She seemed to me then amazingly rich and mature and yet sweet. She was like a pear, soft and full-juiced and overflowing with passion. Beside her Hilda seemed like an empty eggshell.

I stayed with the Hartmans that night and the next. There were still three days to go before the Kersch job began. Then I stayed another night. I telegraphed Hilda, 'Delayed. Returning certain tomorrow.'

I never went. I was bound, heart and soul to Blanche Hartman. There was never any getting away from it. I was so far gone that it was not until the second day of that second visit that I noticed the name Hartman* at all.

'I'm going to stay here,' I said to Blanche. 'Lodge here and live with you. Do you want me?'

'Arthur, Arthur.'

'My God,' I said. 'Don't.' I simply couldn't bear the repetition of my name. It awoke every sort of fierce passion in me.

Then after a time I said: 'There's something I've got to tell you.'

'I know,' she said. 'About another girl. It doesn't matter. I don't want to hear. I could tell you about other men.'

'No, but listen,' I said. 'I'm married.' I told her all about Hilda.

'It doesn't matter,' she said. 'It makes no difference. You could be a Mormon* and it wouldn't matter.'

And after that, because it mattered nothing to her, it mattered nothing to me. There is no conscience in passion. When I did think of Hilda and the Brownsons it was like the squirt of a syphon on to a blazing furnace. I really had no conscience at all. I walked out of one life into another as easily as from one room into another.

The only difficulty was Kersch and Co. It was there that Hilda would enquire for me as soon as I failed to turn up.

Actually I got out of the Kersch difficulty as easily as I got out of the rest. I didn't go back there either.

I went on living with Blanche until the war* broke out. I got another job. Electrical engineers were scarcer in those days. Then, as soon as the war broke out, I joined up.

In a way it was almost a relief. Passion can go too far and one can have too much of it. I was tired out by a life that was too full of sublimity. It was not that I was tired of Blanche. She remained as irresistible to me as when I had first seen her in the green and orange kimono. It was only that I was tired of the constant act of passion itself. My spirit, as it were, had gone stale and I needed rest.

The war gave it to me. As soon as I came home for my first leave I knew it was the best thing that could have happened to me. Blanche and I went straight back to the almost unearthly plane of former intimacy. It was the old almost catastrophic ecstasy.

I say almost catastrophic. Now, when I think of it, I see that it was really catastrophic. One cannot expect a woman to feed off the food of the gods and then suddenly, because one man among a million is not there, to go back on a diet of nothing at all. I am trying to be reasonable about this. I am not blaming Blanche. It is the ecstasy between us that I am blaming. It could not have been otherwise than catastrophic.

I always think it odd that I did not see the catastrophe coming before it did. But perhaps if I had seen it coming it would have ceased to be a catastrophe. I don't know. I only know that I came home in 1917, unexpectedly, and found that Blanche was carrying on with another man.

I always remembered that Mrs Hartman looked extraordinarily scared as I walked into the shop that day. She was an assured, masterful woman and it was not at all like her to be scared. After a minute or so I went upstairs and in my bedroom a man was just buttoning up his waistcoat. Blanche was not there, but I understood.

I was furious, but the fury did not last. Blanche shattered it. She was a woman to whom passion was as essential as bread. She reminded me of that. But she reminded me also of something else. She reminded me that I was not married to her.

'But the moral obligation!' I raged.

'It's no good,' she said. 'I can't help it. It's no more than kissing to me. Don't be angry, honey. If you can't take me as I am you're not bound to take me at all.'

And in the end she melted my fury. 'What's between us is different from all the rest,' she said. I believed her and she demonstrated it to me too. And I clung to that until the end of the war.

But when I came home finally it had gone further than that. There was more than one man. They came to the shop, travellers in the sweet-trade, demobilised young officers with cars. They called while I was at my job.

I found out about it. This time I didn't say anything. I did something instead. I gave up what the Brownsons would have called my appointment.

'But what have you done that for?' Blanche said.

'I can't stand being tied by a job any more,' I said. 'I'll work here. We'll develop the shop. There's money in it.'

'Who's going to pay for it?'

'I will.'

Just before I married Hilda I had nearly a hundred and fifty pounds in the bank. I had had it transferred to a London branch and it was almost all of it still there. I drew it out and in the summer of 1919 I spent nearly £80 of it on renovating the Hartmans' shop. Blanche was delighted. She supervised the decorations and the final colour scheme of the combined shop and café was orange and green.

'Like your kimono,' I said. 'You remember it? That old one?'

'Oh! Arthur. I've still got it.'

'Put it on,' I said.

She went upstairs and put it on. In about a minute I followed her. It was like old times. It brought us together again.

'Tell me something,' I said. 'That first day, when I came in. You hadn't anything on underneath, had you?'

'No,' she said. 'I'd just had a bath and it was all I had time to slip on.'

'By God, kiss me.'

She kissed me and I held her very tight. Her body was thicker and heavier now, but she was still lovely. It was all I asked. I was quite happy.

Then something else happened. I got used to seeing men in the shop. Most of them shot off now when they saw me, but one day when I came back from the bank there was a man in the living-room. He was an oldish chap, with pepper and salt hair cut rather short.

'Hello,' I said, 'what's eating you?' I got to be rather short with any man I saw hanging about the place.

'Nothing's eating me,' he said. 'It's me who wants something to eat.'

'Oh! Who are you?'

'My name's Hartman,' he said.

I looked straight at his hair. It was Blanche's father. And in a minute I knew that he was out of prison.

I don't know why, but it was more of a shock to me than Blanche's affairs with other men. Blanche and I could fight out the question of unfaithfulness between ourselves, but the question of a criminal in the house was different.

'He isn't a criminal,' Blanche said. 'He's easily led and he was led away by others. Be kind to him, honey.'

Perhaps I was soft. Perhaps I had no right to do anything. It was not my house, it was not my father. Blanche was not even my wife. What could I possibly do but let him stay?

That summer we did quite well with the new café. We made a profit of nine and very often ten or eleven pounds a week. Hartman came home in May. In July things began to get worse. Actually, with the summer at its height, they ought to have been better. But the takings dropped to six and even five pounds. Blanche and her mother kept saying that they couldn't understand it.

But I could. Or at least I could after a long time. It was Hartman. He was not only sponging on me, but robbing the till too. All the hard-earned savings of the shop were being boozed away by Hartman.

I wanted to throw him out. But Blanche and her mother wouldn't hear of it. 'He's nothing but a damned scoundrel,' I shouted.

'He's my father,' Blanche said.

That was the beginning of it. I date the antagonism between us and also the estrangement between us from that moment. It was never the same afterwards. I could stand Blanche being nothing more or less than a whore, but it was the thought of the old man and the thought of my own stupidity and folly that enraged me and finally almost broke me up.

Perhaps I shouldn't have written the word whore, and I wouldn't have done if it wasn't for the fact that, as I sit here, my heart is really almost broken.

I am sitting in what used to be my bedroom. We have changed it into a sitting-room now. We ought to have it done up. We haven't had new paper on it for seven or eight years.

I am just fifty. I think Blanche is just about fifty, too. She is out somewhere. It's no use thinking where. Passion is still as essential to her as bread. It means no more to her and I have long since given up asking where she goes. And somehow – and this is the damnable part of it all – I am still very fond of her, but gently and rather foolishly now. What I feel for her most is regret. Not anger and not passion. I couldn't keep up with her pace. She long since outdistanced me in the matter of emotions.

Mrs Hartman is dead. I am sorry. She was likeable and though sometimes I didn't trust her I think she liked me. Hartman still hangs on. I keep the till money locked up, but somehow he picks the locks, and there it is. He's too clever for me and I can't prove it. I feel as if, now, I am in a prison far more complete than any Hartman was ever in. It is a bondage directly inherited from that first catastrophic passion for Blanche. It's that, really, that I can't escape. It binds me irrevocably, I know that I shall never escape.

Last night, for instance, I had a chance to escape. I know of course that I'm a free man and that I am not married to Blanche and that I could walk out now and never come back. But this was different.

Hilda asked for me. I was in the shop, alone, just about six o'clock. I was looking at the paper. We don't get many people in the café now, but I always have the evening paper, in case. This district has gone down a lot and the café of course has gone down with it. We don't get the people in that we did. And as I was reading the paper the wireless was on. At six o'clock the dance band ended, and in another moment or two someone was saying my name.

'Will Arthur Lawson, last heard of in London twenty-five years ago, go at once to the Nottingham Infirmary, where his wife, Hilda Lawson, is dangerously ill.'

That was all. No one but me, in this house I mean, heard it. Afterwards no one mentioned it. Round here they think my name is Hartman. It was as though it had never happened.

But it was for me all right. When I heard it I stood dumb, as though something had struck me down. I almost died where I stood, at the foot of the stairs.

Then after a bit I got over it enough to walk upstairs to the sitting-room. I did not know quite what I was doing. I felt faint and I sat down. I thought it over. After a minute I could see that there was no question of going. If it had been Blanche – yes. But not Hilda. I could not face it. And I just sat there and thought not of what I should do but what I might have done.

I thought of that hot day in 1911, and the Kersch job and how glad I was to get it. I thought about Hilda. I wondered what she looked like now and what she had done with herself for twenty-five years and what she had suffered. Finally I thought of that catastrophic ecstasy with Blanche, and then of the kimono. And I wondered how things might have gone if the Hartmans' ice-cream freezer had never broken and if Blanche had been dressed as any other girl would have been dressed that day.

And thinking and wondering, I sat there and cried like a child.

NOTES

Congregationalists (p64)

members of a Protestant church organization (now part of the United Reformed Church)

up West (p65)

to the West End, the area of London where the night-life is (theatres, cinemas, restaurants, clubs, etc.)

fast (p67)

(old-fashioned, informal) sexually inviting

keep herself for me (p70)

wait until marriage before having sexual intercourse

Hartman (p77)

this name, like the name Kersch, is probably of Jewish origin

Mormon (p77)

a member of a religious sect founded in New York in 1830, which used to allow a man to have more than one wife

the war (p78)

the First World War, 1914–1918

DISCUSSION

1 'I couldn't help it. I can resist everything except temptation,' says a character in one of Oscar Wilde's plays. Is Arthur Lawson a similar kind of character? Even if he hadn't met Blanche, do you think he probably would have been unfaithful to Hilda sooner or later? Was it just as much Blanche's fault as Arthur's? How important do you think the kimono really was in changing the course of Arthur's life?

2 The rules governing relationships between men and women vary from society to society and from age to age. Was Arthur's behaviour to Hilda inexcusable by any set of rules? Accepting that Arthur was unable to break free of his obsession with Blanche, list the things that he should have done, or should not have done, in relation to Hilda.

3 At the circus Arthur and Blanche go to in the East End, the trapeze artist has a catastrophic failure of nerve. Why do you think this incident is included? What significance does it have for the story?

4 At one point, when Arthur is full of rage at his own 'stupidity and folly', he uses the word 'whore' about Blanche. Do you think the author presents Blanche as an immoral or an amoral character?

5 When Arthur heard the message about his dying wife, he decided that he could not go because he 'could not face it'. What do *you* think he should have done?

LANGUAGE FOCUS

1 Rephrase these expressions from the story in your own words.

> *I would go up West and do myself rather well.*   (p65)
> *Wade's Hotel. No. That beats me.*   (p66)
> *Come up and see it. It won't eat you.*   *(p69)*
> *I ought to have broken it off with Hilda at once.*   (p75)
> *I talked round Hilda, and Hilda talked round her mother*   (p76)
> *I was so far gone*   (p77)
> *as soon as the war broke out, I joined up*   (p78)
> *Blanche was carrying on with another man*   (p78)
> *Most of them shot off now when they saw me*   (p80)
> *What's eating you?*   (p80)
> *I got to be rather short with any man I saw hanging about the place.*   (p80)
> *He was not only sponging on me*   (p81)
> *This district has gone down a lot*   (p82)

ACTIVITIES

1 Suppose that Arthur never went home after his first weekend with Blanche, and wrote to Hilda to break off their engagement. Write his letter for him, keeping it as short and as apologetic as possible. Do you think he should mention 'another woman', or should he invent some other, possibly less hurtful, explanation?

2 Write a short report on Hilda Lawson's life for a local newspaper after her death, using only the information (or lack of it) that Hilda herself had. Include some speculation about her missing husband's failure to respond to the wireless appeal. (He might, for example, easily have been killed in the 1914–18 war.)

3 Is *The Kimono* a good title for this story? What other titles might be appropriate? Think of titles which would convey the ideas of obsession, or a catastrophic turning-point in someone's life, or a moral judgement on the main character's behaviour.

A SHOCKING ACCIDENT

THE AUTHOR

Graham Greene was born in 1904. Educated at Oxford University, he then worked for various newspapers, was an intelligence agent in the Second World War, and frequently travelled in remote and dangerous places. He wrote novels, short stories, plays, and travel books. Among his lighter novels, which Greene called 'entertainments', are *Stamboul Train*, *A Gun for Sale*, *Our Man in Havana*, and *The Third Man*, which was made into a famous film. Greene himself preferred his other novels, which reflect his intense interest in religious and moral issues (he was a Roman Catholic convert). These powerful and sombre novels include *Brighton Rock*, *The Power and the Glory*, *The End of the Affair*, *The Heart of the Matter*, *A Burnt-out Case*, and *The Human Factor*. Greene died in 1991.

THE STORY

Humour is a two-edged sword. People who lack a sense of humour can be dreary company, but a misplaced sense of humour – laughing at the wrong thing, at the wrong time, in the wrong place – can cause havoc. 'Nothing spoils a romance so much as a sense of humour in the woman,' wrote Oscar Wilde.

Romance lies in the future for Jerome, who at the moment is only nine, and still at school. He is sitting solemn and wide-eyed in front of his housemaster's desk, about to be given news of his absent and adored father. It is not good news and Mr Wordsworth plays with the ruler on his desk, at a loss for words. He also seems to be having a terrible struggle with the muscles of his face . . .

A SHOCKING ACCIDENT

I

Jerome was called into his housemaster's* room in the break between the second and the third class on a Thursday morning. He had no fear of trouble, for he was a warden – the name that the proprietor and headmaster of a rather expensive preparatory school* had chosen to give to approved, reliable boys in the lower forms (from a warden one became a guardian and finally before leaving, it was hoped for Marlborough or Rugby*, a crusader). The housemaster, Mr Wordsworth, sat behind his desk with an appearance of perplexity and apprehension. Jerome had the odd impression when he entered that he was a cause of fear.

'Sit down, Jerome,' Mr Wordsworth said. 'All going well with the trigonometry?'

'Yes, sir.'

'I've had a telephone call, Jerome. From your aunt. I'm afraid I have bad news for you.'

'Yes, sir?'

'Your father has had an accident.'

'Oh.'

Mr Wordsworth looked at him with some surprise. 'A serious accident.'

'Yes, sir?'

Jerome worshipped his father: the verb is exact. As man re-creates God, so Jerome re-created his father – from a restless widowed author into a mysterious adventurer who travelled in far places – Nice, Beirut, Majorca, even the Canaries*. The time had arrived about his eighth birthday when Jerome believed that his father either 'ran guns' or was a member of the British Secret Service. Now it occurred to him that his father might have been wounded in 'a hail of machine-gun bullets'.

Mr Wordsworth played with the ruler on his desk. He seemed at a loss how to continue. He said, 'You know your father was in Naples?'

'Yes, sir.'

'Your aunt heard from the hospital today.'

'Oh.'

Mr Wordsworth said with desperation, 'It was a street accident.'

'Yes, sir?' It seemed quite likely to Jerome that they would call it a street accident. The police of course had fired first; his father would not take human life except as a last resort.

'I'm afraid your father was very seriously hurt indeed.'

'Oh.'

'In fact, Jerome, he died yesterday. Quite without pain.'

'Did they shoot him through the heart?'

'I beg your pardon. What did you say, Jerome?'

'Did they shoot him through the heart?'

'Nobody shot him, Jerome. A pig fell on him.' An inexplicable convulsion took place in the nerves of Mr Wordsworth's face; it really looked for a moment as though he were going to laugh. He closed his eyes, composed his features and said rapidly as though it were necessary to expel the story as rapidly as possible, 'Your father was walking along a street in Naples when a pig fell on him. A shocking accident. Apparently in the poorer quarters of Naples they keep pigs on their balconies. This one was on the fifth floor. It had grown too fat. The balcony broke. The pig fell on your father.'

Mr Wordsworth left his desk rapidly and went to the window, turning his back on Jerome. He shook a little with emotion.

Jerome said, 'What happened to the pig?'

2

This was not callousness on the part of Jerome, as it was interpreted by Mr Wordsworth to his colleagues (he even discussed with them whether, perhaps, Jerome was yet fitted to be a warden). Jerome was only attempting to visualize the strange scene to get the details right. Nor was Jerome a boy who cried; he was a boy who brooded, and it never occurred to him at his preparatory school that the circumstances of his father's death were comic – they were still part of the mystery of life. It was later, in his first term at his public school, when he told the story to his best friend, that he began to realize how it affected others. Naturally after that disclosure he was known, rather unreasonably, as Pig.

Unfortunately his aunt had no sense of humour. There was an enlarged snapshot of his father on the piano; a large sad man in an unsuitable dark suit posed in Capri with an umbrella (to guard him against sunstroke), the Faraglione rocks forming the background. By the age of sixteen Jerome was well aware that the portrait looked more like the author of *Sunshine and Shade* and *Rambles in the Balearics* than an agent of the Secret Service. All the same he loved the memory of his father: he still possessed an album fitted with picture-postcards (the stamps had been soaked off long ago for his other collection), and it pained him when his aunt embarked with strangers on the story of his father's death.

'A shocking accident,' she would begin, and the stranger would compose his or her features into the correct shape for interest and commiseration. Both reactions, of course, were false, but it was terrible for Jerome to see how suddenly, midway in her rambling discourse, the interest would become genuine. 'I can't think how such things can be allowed in a civilized country,' his aunt would say. 'I suppose one has to regard Italy as civilized. One is prepared for all kinds of things abroad, of course, and my brother was a great traveller. He always carried a water-filter with him. It was far less expensive, you know, than buying all those bottles of mineral water. My brother always said that his filter paid for his dinner wine. You can see from that what a careful man he was, but who could possibly have expected when he was walking along the Via Dottore Manuele Panucci on his way to the Hydrographic Museum that a pig would fall on him?' That was the moment when the interest became genuine.

Jerome's father had not been a very distinguished writer, but the time always seems to come, after an author's death, when somebody thinks it worth his while to write a letter to the *Times Literary Supplement* announcing the preparation of a biography and asking to see any letters or documents or receive any anecdotes from friends of the dead man. Most of the biographies, of course, never appear – one wonders whether the whole thing may not be an obscure form of blackmail and whether many a potential writer of a biography or thesis finds the means in this way to finish his education at Kansas or Nottingham. Jerome, however, as a chartered accountant, lived far from the literary world. He did not realize how small the menace really was, or that the danger period for someone of his father's obscurity had long passed. Sometimes he rehearsed the method of recounting his father's death so as to reduce the comic element to its smallest dimensions – it would be of no use to refuse information, for in that case the biographer would undoubtedly visit his aunt, who was living to a great old age with no sign of flagging.

It seemed to Jerome that there were two possible methods – the first led gently up to the accident, so that by the time it was described the listener was so well prepared that the death came really as an anti-climax. The chief danger of laughter in such a story was always surprise. When he rehearsed this method Jerome began boringly enough.

'You know Naples and those high tenement buildings? Somebody once told me that the Neapolitan always feels at home in New York just as the man from Turin feels at home in London because the river runs in much the same way in both cities. Where was I? Oh, yes. Naples, of course. You'd be surprised in the poorer quarters what things they keep on the balconies of those sky-scraping tenements – not washing, you know, or bedding, but things like livestock, chickens or even pigs. Of course the pigs get no exercise whatever and fatten all the quicker.' He could imagine how his hearer's eyes would have glazed by this time. 'I've no idea, have you, how heavy a pig can be, but these old buildings are all badly in need of repair. A balcony on the fifth floor gave way under one of those pigs. It struck the third floor balcony on its way down and sort of ricochetted into the street. My father was on the way to the Hydrographic Museum when the pig hit him. Coming from that height and that angle it broke his neck.' This was really a masterly attempt to make an intrinsically interesting subject boring.

The other method Jerome rehearsed had the virtue of brevity.

'My father was killed by a pig.'

'Really? In India?'

'No, in Italy.'

'How interesting. I never realized there was pig-sticking* in Italy. Was your father keen on polo?'

In course of time, neither too early nor too late, rather as though, in his capacity as a chartered accountant, Jerome had studied the statistics and taken the average, he became engaged to be married: to a pleasant fresh-faced girl of twenty-five whose father was a doctor in Pinner*. Her name was Sally, her favourite author was still Hugh Walpole*, and she had adored babies ever since she had been given a doll at the age of five which moved its eyes and made water. Their relationship was contented rather than exciting, as became the love-affair of a chartered accountant; it would never have done if it had interfered with the figures.

One thought worried Jerome, however. Now that within a year he might himself become a father, his love for the dead man increased; he realized what affection had gone into the picture-postcards. He felt a longing to protect his memory, and uncertain whether this quiet love of his would survive if Sally were so insensitive as to laugh when she heard the story of his father's death. Inevitably she would hear it when Jerome brought her to dinner with his aunt. Several times he tried to tell her himself, as she was naturally anxious to know all she could that concerned him.

'You were very small when your father died?'

'Just nine.'

'Poor little boy,' she said.

'I was at school. They broke the news to me.'

'Did you take it very hard?'

'I can't remember.'

'You never told me how it happened.'

'It was very sudden. A street accident.'

'You'll never drive fast, will you, Jemmy?' (She had begun to call him 'Jemmy'.) It was too late then to try the second method – the one he thought of as the pig-sticking one.

They were going to marry quietly in a registry-office and have their honeymoon at Torquay. He avoided taking her to see his aunt until a week before the wedding, but then the night came and he could not have told himself whether his apprehension was more for his father's memory or the security of his own love.

The moment came all too soon. 'Is that Jemmy's father?' Sally asked, picking up the portrait of the man with the umbrella.

'Yes, dear. How did you guess?'

'He has Jemmy's eyes and brow, hasn't he?'

'Has Jerome lent you his books?'

'No.'

'I will give you a set for your wedding. He wrote so tenderly about his travels. My own favourite is *Nooks and Crannies*. He would have had a great future. It made that shocking accident all the worse.'

'Yes?'

Jerome longed to leave the room and not see that loved face crinkle with irresistible amusement.

'I had so many letters from his readers after the pig fell on him.' She had never been so abrupt before.

And then the miracle happened. Sally did not laugh. Sally sat with open eyes of horror while his aunt told her the story, and at the end, 'How horrible,' Sally said. 'It makes you think, doesn't it? Happening like that. Out of a clear sky.'

Jerome's heart sang with joy. It was as though she had appeased his fear for ever. In the taxi going home he kissed her with more passion than he had ever shown and she returned it. There were babies in her pale blue pupils, babies that rolled their eyes and made water.

'A week today,' Jerome said, and she squeezed his hand. 'Penny for your thoughts, my darling.'

'I was wondering,' Sally said, 'what happened to the poor pig?'

'They almost certainly had it for dinner,' Jerome said happily and kissed the dear child again.

NOTES

housemaster   (p87)

     a teacher in charge of a group of children (a 'house') in a school

preparatory school   (p87)

     a private (fee-paying) school for children up to the age of 13

Marlborough, Rugby   (p87)

     well-known public (fee-paying) schools for children aged 13 and above

Canaries   (p87)

     the Canary Islands, off the north-west coast of Africa

pig-sticking   (p91)

     the hunting of wild boar (pigs) with a spear on horseback

Pinner   (p91)

     a district on the outskirts of London

Hugh Walpole   (p91)

     a writer in the early 1900s, whose novels were very popular but not considered to be of 'literary' status

DISCUSSION

1   There are two kinds of love in this story: the love of a boy for his father, and the love between a young man and a young woman. Do you think the author treats these relationships sympathetically despite the comic element to the story, or do you find the humour callous, or trivializing?

2   Jerome worships his father and creates an elaborate fantasy about him. Is this a normal thing to do in childhood? Why do children do it? In later life, Jerome realizes that his father was not the exotic, glamorous figure of boys' adventure stories. Did that diminish his affection for his father? What does that tell us about Jerome himself?

3   The idea of someone being killed by a falling pig seems rather surreal. Did people find it funny because there is something intrinsically comic about the pig itself? In what contexts do we use the expression, 'And pigs might fly'? Why pigs, and not donkeys, for example? Would it have been equally comic if a large dog had fallen on Jerome's father?

LANGUAGE FOCUS

1   *Jerome had the odd impression when he entered that he was a cause of fear.*

In the light of what the housemaster has to say to him, how do you account for Jerome's impression?

2   *He shook a little with emotion.*
    What kind of emotion do you think Mr Wordsworth was shaking with?

3   *'In fact, Jerome, he died yesterday. Quite without pain.'*
    'Did they shoot him through the heart?'
    Jerome's reply seemed very appropriate to him, but very inappropriate
    to Mr Wordsworth. Why? What effect does this mis-match have?

4   There are two misunderstandings about the tale of Jerome's father's
    death, which follow these two statements by Jerome:
    'My father was killed by a pig.' (p91)
    'It was very sudden. A street accident.' (p92)
    Explain how the responses to these statements show what assumptions
    the listeners were making. Do you think these were reasonable or likely
    assumptions for the listeners to make? What would you have assumed?

5   Imagine that Jerome had told the story like this:
    My father was killed in an accident in Naples. He was walking down
    a street when a balcony broke off a building just above him.
    What is the likely assumption that listeners would make here? Think
    of some other ways of telling the story which, by omitting some details
    and focussing on others, would avoid the comic element.

ACTIVITIES

1   Imagine that Jerome keeps a diary. Write his entries for these three days:
    a) the day he learnt of his father's death
    b) the day he told his best friend how his father died
    c) the day Sally learnt how his father died.

2   The story has quite a light-hearted ending. Instead of
    And then the miracle happened. Sally did not laugh.
    try writing a new ending, beginning with
    And then it happened. Sally laughed.
    How will you continue? Will Jerome be sad but resigned, furious with
    his aunt, deeply hurt? Will he explain his problem to Sally, say nothing,
    break off his engagement? How much does your new ending change the
    mood of the story? Is the humour still there, or has it changed into
    something else? Which ending do you prefer, and why?

Horrors of the Road

The Author

Fay Weldon was born in Worcester in 1933, but was raised in a family of women in New Zealand. Returning to Britain, she studied economics and psychology, and worked in advertising before turning to writing. She has written many plays for radio, the stage, and television, the most well-known being *Upstairs, Downstairs* and her adaptation of Jane Austen's *Pride and Prejudice*. Among her novels are *The Fat Woman's Joke, Female Friends, Praxis, The Life and Loves of a She Devil, The Cloning of Joanna May,* and *Growing Rich*. Short-story collections include *Wicked Women* and *A Hard Time to be a Father*. Her writing expresses a contemporary feminist consciousness and is often sharply satirical about male-dominated society.

The Story

Loyalty is a commendable virtue, whether to a friend, a worthy cause, a husband, a wife. But when should it stop? Can you have too much of it? Can it become counter-productive? In a much-quoted line from Shakespeare, Hamlet's mother, watching the Player Queen declare loyal and undying love for her King, says uneasily to Hamlet, 'The lady doth protest too much, methinks.'

Piers' wife is confined to a wheelchair. Her legs simply don't work any longer, she tells the psychotherapist, and proudly declares that she is a great mystery to the doctors. But there seems to be no mystery about her devotion to her husband. Piers is a famous and successful scientist, and so clever, so good-looking, such a wonderful companion in thirty years of holidaying in France . . .

Horrors of the Road

Miss Jacobs, I don't believe in psychotherapy. I really do think it's a lot of nonsense. Now it's taken me considerable nerve to say that – I'm a rather mild person and hate to be thought rude. I just wouldn't want to be here under false pretences: it wouldn't be fair to you, would it?

But Piers wants me to come and see you, so of course I will. He's waiting outside in your pretty drawing-room: I said he should go, and come back when the session was up: that I'd be perfectly all right but he likes to be at hand in case anything happens. Just sometimes I do fall forward, out of my chair – so far I haven't hurt myself. Once it was face-first into a feather sofa; the second was trickier – I was with Martin – he's my little grandchild, you know, David's boy, the only one so far – at the sandpit in the park and I just pitched forward into the sand. Someone sent for an ambulance but it wasn't really necessary – I was perfectly all right, instantly. Well, except for this one big permanent fact that my legs don't work.

I'm a great mystery to the doctors. Piers has taken me everywhere – Paris, New York, Tokyo – but the verdict seems to be the same: it's all in my head. It is a hysterical paralysis. I find this humiliating: as if I'd done it on purpose just to be a nuisance. I'm the last person in the world to be a nuisance!

Did you see Piers? Isn't he handsome? He's in his mid-fifties, you know, but so good-looking. Of course he has an amazing brain – well, the whole world knows that – and I think that helps to keep people looking young. I have a degree in Economics myself – unusual for a housewife of my age – but of course I stayed home to devote myself to Piers and the children. I think, on the whole, women should do that. Don't you? Why don't you answer my questions? Isn't that what you're supposed to do? Explain me to myself? No?

I must explain myself to myself! Oh.

Behind every great man stands a woman. I believe that. Piers is a Nobel Prize* winner. Would he have done it without me? I expect so. He just wouldn't have had me, would he, or the four children? They're all doing very well. Piers was away quite a lot when the children were young – he's a particle physicist, as I'm sure you know. He had to be away. They don't keep cyclotrons* in suitably domestic places, and the money had to be earned somehow. But we all always had these holidays together in France. How we loved France. How well we knew it. Piers would drive; I'd navigate; the four children piled in the back. Of course these days we fly. There's just Piers and me. It's glamorous and exciting, and people know who he is so the service is good. Waiters don't mind so much . . . Mind what? . . . I thought you weren't supposed to ask questions. I was talking about holidays, in the past, long ago. Well, not so long ago. We went on till the youngest was fifteen; Brutus that is, and he's only twenty now. Can it be only five years?

I miss those summer dockside scenes: the cars lined up at dusk or dawn waiting for the ferry home: sunburned families, careless and exhausted after weeks in the sun. By careless I don't mean without care – just without caring any more. They'll sleep all night in their cars to be first in the queue for the ferry, and not worry about it; on the journey out they'd have gone berserk. Brown faces and brittle blonde hair and grubby children; and the roof-racks with the tents and the water cans and the boxes of wine and strings of garlic.

Volvos and Cortinas and Volkswagen vans. Of course our cars never looked smart: we even started out once with a new one, but by the time we came back it was dented and bumped and battered. French drivers are so dreadful, aren't they; and their road signs are impossible.

How did the paralysis start? It was completely unexpected. There were no warning signs – no numbness, no dizziness, nothing like that. It was our thirtieth wedding anniversary. To celebrate we were going to do a tour of France in Piers' new MG*. It can do 110 mph, you know, but Piers doesn't often go at more than fifty-five – that's the speed limit in the States, you know, and he says they know what they're doing – it's the best speed for maximum safety – but he likes to have cars that can go fast. To get out of trouble in an emergency, Piers says. We were going on the Weymouth/Cherbourg route – I'm usually happier with Dover/Calais – the sea journey's shorter for one thing, and somehow the longer the journey through England the more likely Piers is to forget to drive on the right once we're in France. I've noticed it. But I don't argue about things like that. Piers knows what he's doing – I never backseat drive. I'm his wife, he's my husband. We love each other.

So we were setting out for Weymouth, the bags were packed, the individual route maps from the AA* in the glove compartment – they'd arrived on time, for once (I'd taken a Valium* in good time – my heart tends to beat rather fast, almost to the point of palpitations, when I'm navigating.) I was wearing a practical non-crease dress – you know what long journeys are like – you always end up a little stained. Piers loves melons and likes me to feed him wedges as we drive along – and you know how ripe a ripe French melon can be. Piers will spend hours choosing one from a market stall. He'll test every single one on display – you know, sniffing and pressing the ends for just the right degree of tenderness – until he's found one that's absolutely perfect. Sometimes, before he's satisfied, he'll go through the fruit boxes at the back of the stall as well. The French like you to be particular, Piers says. They'll despise you if you accept just anything. And then, of course, if the melon's not to go over the top, they have to be eaten quite quickly – in the car as often as not . . .

Anyway, as I was saying, I was about to step into the car when my legs just kind of folded and I sank down on to the pavement, and that was six months ago, and I haven't walked since. No, no palpitations since either. I can't remember if I had palpitations before I was married – I've been married for ever!

And there was no holiday. Just me paralysed. No tour of France. Beautiful France. I adore the Loire and the châteaux, don't you? The children loved the West Coast: those stretches of piny woods and the long, long beaches and the great Atlantic rollers – but after the middle of August the winds change and everything gets dusty and somehow grizzly. When the children were small we camped, but every year the sites got more formal and more crowded and more full of *frites** and Piers didn't like that. He enjoyed what he called 'wilderness camping'. In the camping guides which describe the sites there's always an area section – that is, the area allowed for each tent. Point five of a hectare is crowded: two hectares perfectly possible. Piers liked ten hectares, which meant a hillside somewhere and no television room for the children or *frites* stall – and that meant more work for me, not that I grudged it: a change of venue for cooking – such lovely portable calor gas stoves we had: you could do a three-course meal on just two burners if you were clever, if the wind wasn't too high – is as good as a rest from cooking. It was just that the children preferred the crowded sites, and I did sometimes think they were better for the children's French. An English sparrow and a French sparrow sing pretty much the same song. But there you are, Piers loved the wilderness. He'd always measure the actual hectarage available for our tent, and if it didn't coincide with what was in the book would take it up with the relevant authorities. I remember it once ending up with people having to move their tents at ten in the evening to make proper room for ours – we'd driven three hundred miles that day and Brutus was only two. That wasn't Piers' fault: it was the camp proprietor's. Piers merely knocked him up to point out that our site wasn't the dimension it ought to be, and he over-reacted quite dreadfully. I was glad to get away from that site in the morning, I can tell you. It really wasn't Piers' fault; just one of those things. I'm glad it was only a stop-over. The other campers just watched us go, in complete silence. It was weird. And Fanny cried all the way to Poitiers.

Such a tearful little thing, Fanny. Piers liked to have a picnic lunch at about three o'clock – the French roads clear at midday while everyone goes off to gorge themselves on lunch, so you can make really good time wherever you're going. Sometimes I did wonder where it was we *were* going to, or *why* we had to make such time, but on the other hand those wonderful white empty B-roads, poplar-lined, at a steady 55 mph . . . anyway, we'd buy our lunch at midday – wine and pâté and long French bread and Orangina for the children, and then at three start looking for a nice place to picnic. Nothing's harder! If the place is right, the traffic's wrong. Someone's on your tail hooting – how those French drivers do hoot – they can see the GB plates – they know it means the driver's bound to forget and go round roundabouts the wrong way – and before you know it the ideal site is passed. The ideal site has a view, no snakes, some sun and some shade, and I like to feel the car's right off the road – especially if it's a Route Nationale* – though Piers doesn't worry too much. Once actually some idiot did drive right into it – he didn't brake in time – but as Piers had left our car in gear, and not put on the handbrake or anything silly, it just shot forward and not much damage was done. How is it that other cars always look so smooth and somehow new? I suppose their owners must just keep them in garages all the time having the bumps knocked out and re-sprays – well, fools and their money are often parted, as Piers keeps saying.

What was I talking about? Stopping for lunch. Sometimes it would be 4.30 before we found somewhere really nice, and by four you could always rely on Fanny to start crying. I'd give her water from the Pschitt* bottle – how the children giggled – Pschitt – every year a ritual, lovely giggle – and break off bread from the loaf for her, but still she grizzled: and Daddy would stop and start and stare over hedges and go a little way down lanes and find them impossible and back out onto the main road, and the children would fall silent, except for Fanny. Aren't French drivers rude? Had you noticed? I'd look sideways at a passing car and the driver would be staring at us, screwing his thumb into his head, or pretending to slit his throat with his finger – and always these honks and hoots, and once someone pulled in and forced us to stop and tried to drag poor Piers out of the car, goodness knows why. Just general Gallic over-excitement, I suppose. Piers is a wonderfully safe driver. I do think he sometimes inconveniences other cars the way he stops at intersections – you know how muddling their road signs are, especially on city ring roads, and how they seem to be telling you to go right or left when actually they mean straight on. And Piers is a scientist – he likes to be sure he's doing the right thing. I have the maps; I do my best: I memorize whole areas of the country, so I will know when passing through, say, Limoges, on the way from Périgueux to Issoudun, and have to make lightning decisions – Piers

seems to speed up in towns. No! Not the Tulle road, not the
Clermont road, not the Montluçon but the Châteauroux road. Only
the Châteauroux road isn't marked! Help! What's its number? Dear
God, it's the N20! We'll die! The N147 to Bellac then, and cut
through on the B-roads to Argenton, La Châtre . . . So look for the
Poitiers sign. Bellac's on the road to Poitiers—

So he stops, if he's not convinced I'm right, and takes the map
himself and studies it before going on. Which meant, in later years,
finding his magnifying glass. He hates spectacles! And you know
what those overhead traffic lights are like in small country towns,
impossible to see, so no one takes any notice of them! Goodness
knows how French drivers survive at all. We had one or two nasty
misses through no fault of our own every holiday; I did in the end
feel happier if I took Valium. But I never liked Piers to know I was
taking it – it seemed a kind of statement of lack of faith – which
is simply untrue. Look at the way he carried me in, cradled me in
his arms, laid me on this sofa! I trust him implicitly. I am his wife.
He is my husband.

What was I saying? Fanny grizzling. She took off to New Zealand
as soon as she'd finished her college course. A long way away.
Almost as far as she could get, I find myself saying, I don't know
why. I know she loves us and we certainly love her. She writes
frequently. David's a racing car driver. Piers and I are very upset
about this. Such a dangerous occupation. Those cars get up to 200
mph – and Piers did so hate speed. Angela's doing psychiatric
nursing. They say she has a real gift for it.

I remember once I said to Piers – we were on the ring road round
Angers – turn left here, meaning the T-junction we were
approaching – but he swung straight left across the other

carriageway, spying a little side road there – empty because all the traffic was round the corner, held up by the lights, ready to surge foward. He realized what he'd done, and stopped, leaving us broadside across the main road. 'Reverse!' I shrieked, breaking my rule about no backseat driving, and he did, and we were just out of the way when the expected wall of traffic bore down. 'You should have said second left,' he said, 'that was very nearly a multiple pile-up!' You can't be too careful in France. They're mad drivers, as everyone knows. And with the children in the car too—

But it was all such fun. Piers always knew how to get the best out of waiters and chefs. He'd go right through the menu with the waiter, asking him to explain each dish. If the waiter couldn't do it – and it's amazing how many waiters can't – he would send for the chef and ask him. It did get a little embarrassing sometimes, if the restaurant was very busy, but as Piers said, the French understand food and really appreciate it if you do too. I can make up my mind in a flash what I want to eat: Piers takes ages. As I say, he hates to get things wrong. We'd usually be last to leave any restaurant we ate in, but Piers doesn't believe in hurrying. As he says, a) it's bad for the digestion and b) they don't mind: they're glad to see us appreciating what they have to offer. So many people don't. French waiters are such a rude breed, don't you think? They always seem to have kind of glassy eyes. Goodness knows what they're like if you're *not* appreciating what they have to offer!

And then wine. Piers believes in sending wine back as well as food. Standards have to be maintained. He doesn't believe in serving red wines chilled in the modern fashion, no matter how new they are. And that a bottle of wine under eight francs is as worth discussing as one at thirty francs. He's always very polite: just sends for the wine waiter to discuss the matter, but of course he doesn't speak

French, so difficulties sometimes arise. Acrimony almost. And this kind of funny silence while we leave.

And always when we paid the bill before leaving our hotel, Piers would check and re-check every item. He's got rather short-sighted over the years: he has to use a magnifying glass. The children and I would sit waiting in the car for up to an hour while they discussed the cost of hot water and what a reasonable profit was, and why it being a fête holiday should make a difference. I do sometimes think, I admit, that Piers has a love/hate relationship with France. He loves the country; he won't go holidaying in Italy or Spain, only France – and yet, you know, those *Dégustation-Libres* that have sprung up all over the place – 'free disgustings', as the children call them – where you taste the wine before choosing? Piers goes in, tastes everything, and if he likes nothing – which is quite often – buys nothing. That, after all, is what they are offering. *Free* wine-tasting. He likes me to go in with him, to taste with him, so that we can compare notes, and I watch the enthusiasm dying in the proprietor's eyes, as he is asked to fetch first this, then that, then the other down from the top shelf, and Piers sips and raises his eyebrows and shakes his head, and then hostility dawns in the shopkeeper's eye, and then boredom, and then I almost think something which borders on derision – and I must tell you, Miss Jacobs, I don't like it, and in the end, whenever we passed a *Dégustation-Libre* and I saw the glint in his eye, and his foot went on the brake – he never looked in his mirror – there was no point, since it was always adjusted to show the car roof – I'd take another Valium – because I think otherwise I would scream, I couldn't help myself. It wasn't that I didn't love and trust and admire Piers, it was the look in the French eye—

Why don't I scream? What are you after? Abreaction*? I know the terms – my daughter Angela's a psychiatric nurse, as I told you, and doing very well. You think I was finally traumatized at the last *Dégustation*? And that's why I can't walk? You'd like to believe that, wouldn't you? I expect you're a feminist – I notice you're wearing a trouser suit – and like to think everything in this world is the man's fault. You want me to scream out tension and rage and terror and horror? I won't! I tell you, France is a joyous place and we all loved those holidays and had some wonderful meals and some knock-out wines, thanks to Piers, and as for his driving, we're all alive, aren't we? Piers, me, David, Angela, Fanny, Brutus. All alive! That must prove something. It's just I don't seem able to walk, and if you would be so kind as to call Piers, he will shift me from your sofa to the chair and wheel me home. Talking will get us nowhere. I do love my husband.

NOTES

Nobel Prize   (p98)

   highly prestigious annual prizes for outstanding international achievement in physics, chemistry, physiology or medicine, literature, economic sciences, and the promotion of peace

cyclotron   (p98)

   an apparatus in physics which examines the behaviour of atomic and subatomic particles when moving at speed

MG   (p99)

   a fashionable make of sports car (MG stands for Morris Garages)

AA   (p99)

   Automobile Association (which provides services for motorists)

Valium   (p99)

   a drug used to reduce anxiety

frites   (p100)

   short for *pommes frites*, the French for fried potatoes ('chips' in British English)

Route Nationale   (p101)

   French for main road or highway

Pschitt   (p102)

   a brand of fizzy drink, pronounced with a silent 'p', which makes it sound like the English swear word 'shit' (hence the children's giggle)

abreaction   (p105)

   a word in psychology meaning the release of a repressed emotion

DISCUSSION

1   We see Piers through his wife's eyes. What impression do we get of him, as a man, a scientist, a father, and a husband? Is he cruel or sadistic, or do you think he is basically well-meaning? What are his main faults? What could his wife have done to make holidays more bearable?

2   Do we ever learn what Piers' wife *really* thinks? Does she believe what she is saying, or is it a desperate attempt to keep up a front to the rest of the world? Why might she be unwilling, or unable, to give a more truthful account of her marriage? Should she be encouraged to give an accurate analysis, or allowed to manage her life in her own way?

3   Did you find this story amusing or sad, or both at the same time? What are the sad aspects, and how are the humorous effects achieved?

Language Focus

1 There are places in the story when Piers' wife is clearly responding to something Miss Jacobs has said. Find these places and decide what Miss Jacobs probably said on each occasion.

2 The irony in this story comes from a narrator whose view of the world differs widely from the true circumstances recognized by the reader. Whether or not Piers' wife believes what she is saying, how do you think the author intends the reader to interpret the following comments? Rewrite them to express what you think is the real meaning.

   • *I miss those summer dockside scenes.* (p98)
   • *Piers knows what he's doing.* (p99)
   • *. . . such lovely portable calor gas stoves we had: you could do a three-course meal on just two burners if you were clever, if the wind wasn't too high.* (p100)
   • *That wasn't Piers' fault: it was the camp proprietor's.* (p101)
   • *Piers is a wonderfully safe driver.* (p102)
   • *Almost as far as she could get, . . . I don't know why.* (p103)
   • *Piers always knew how to get the best out of waiters and chefs.* (p104)

3 When Piers' wife says 'I've been married for ever!', what do you think she means by 'for ever'? Might there be just a hint of criticism here? What other things does she say that contain hints of criticism of Piers?

4 Suppose Piers' wife did 'scream out tension and rage and terror and horror'. What kind of things might she say?

Activities

1 Imagine that you are Miss Jacobs. Write two reports about your session with Piers' wife, each designed for a different reader.
   a) A report for Piers. What could you write that might be helpful to Piers' wife in surviving life with such a husband? How much, if at all, would you hint at the cause of her 'hysterical paralysis'?
   b) A report for a colleague, giving an accurate description of Piers' wife and her relationship with her husband.

2 Imagine that Piers' wife is an assertive, dominant personality, and after a few holidays in France with Piers and the children, she draws up a list of rules for future holidays, dealing with driving, picnics, camp sites, and so on. Write the rules for her.

Ming's Biggest Prey

The Author

Patricia Highsmith was born in 1921 in Texas, and grew up in New York. She decided to become a writer when she was only sixteen. Her first novel, *Strangers on a Train*, was filmed by Alfred Hitchcock, and she went on to write many widely praised novels and collections of short stories. Her books are psychological thrillers, which show us, in a horribly convincing way, the darker side of human nature. Her series of novels about the charming but psychopathic Tom Ripley are particularly famous. Among her best-known titles are *The Talented Mr Ripley* (which was filmed in 1999), *Ripley Under Ground*, *Ripley's Game*, *The Two Faces of January*, and *The Glass Cell*. She died in 1995.

The Story

Strong bonds of affection can exist between humans and domestic pets. Dogs, for example, have been known to pine and starve themselves to death when their owner dies. Cats are usually less demonstrative and more independent, but can also be very sensitive to any threat to their 'territory'. The hunting instincts of the jungle may be diminished by domesticity but have certainly not disappeared.

Ming, like most cats, is principally concerned with his creature comforts – his next meal, a warm and comfortable place to sleep, a little light hunting for entertainment perhaps. His mistress Elaine loves him dearly, an affection which Ming acknowledges and repays with liking. Other human beings are not so favoured, particularly Elaine's friend, the man called Teddie . . .

MING'S BIGGEST PREY

Ming was resting comfortably on the foot of his mistress's bunk, when the man picked him up by the back of the neck, stuck him out on the deck and closed the cabin door. Ming's blue eyes widened in shock and brief anger, then nearly closed again because of the brilliant sunlight. It was not the first time Ming had been thrust out of the cabin rudely, and Ming realized that the man did it when his mistress, Elaine, was not looking.

The sailboat now offered no shelter from the sun, but Ming was not yet too warm. He leapt easily to the cabin roof and stepped on to the coil of rope just behind the mast. Ming liked the rope coil as a couch, because he could see everything from the height, the cup shape of the rope protected him from strong breezes, and also minimized the swaying and sudden changes of angle of the *White Lark*, since it was more or less the centre point. But just now the sail had been taken down, because Elaine and the man had eaten lunch, and often they had a siesta afterward, during which time, Ming knew, that man didn't like him in the cabin. Lunchtime was all right. In fact, Ming had just lunched on delicious grilled fish and a bit of lobster. Now, lying in a relaxed curve on the coil of rope, Ming opened his mouth in a great yawn, then with his slant eyes almost closed against the strong sunlight, gazed at the beige hills and the white and pink houses and hotels that circled the bay of Acapulco. Between the *White Lark* and the shore where people splashed inaudibly, the sun twinkled on the water's surface like thousands of tiny electric lights going on and off. A water-skier went by, skimming up white spray behind him. Such activity! Ming half dozed, feeling the heat of the sun sink into his fur. Ming was from New York, and he considered Acapulco* a great improvement over his environment in the first weeks of his life. He remembered a sunless box with straw on the bottom, three or four other kittens in with him, and a window behind which giant forms paused for a few moments, tried to catch his attention by tapping, then passed on. He did not remember his mother at all. One day a young woman who smelled of something pleasant came into the place and took him away – away from the ugly, frightening smell of dogs, of medicine and parrot dung. Then they went on what Ming now knew was an aeroplane. He was quite used to aeroplanes now and rather liked them. On aeroplanes he sat on Elaine's lap, or slept on her lap, and there were always titbits to eat if he was hungry.

Elaine spent much of the day in a shop in Acapulco, where dresses and slacks and bathing suits hung on all the walls. This place smelled clean and fresh, there were flowers in pots and in boxes out front, and the floor was of cool blue and white tiles. Ming had perfect freedom to wander out into the patio behind the shop, or to sleep in his basket in a corner. There was more sunlight in front of the shop, but mischievous boys often tried to grab him if he sat in front, and Ming could never relax there.

Ming liked best lying in the sun with his mistress on one of the long canvas chairs on their terrace at home. What Ming did not like were the people she sometimes invited to their house, people who spent the night, people by the score who stayed up very late eating and drinking, playing the gramophone or the piano – people who separated him from Elaine. People who stepped on his toes, people who sometimes picked him up from behind before he could do anything about it, so that he had to squirm and fight to get free, people who stroked him roughly, people who closed a door somewhere, locking him in. *People!* Ming detested people. In all the world, he liked only Elaine. Elaine loved him and understood him.

Especially this man called Teddie Ming detested now. Teddie was around all the time lately. Ming did not like the way Teddie looked at him, when Elaine was not watching. And sometimes Teddie, when Elaine was not near, muttered something which Ming knew was a threat. Or a command to leave the room. Ming took it calmly. Dignity was to be preserved. Besides, wasn't his mistress on his side? The man was the intruder. When Elaine was watching, the man sometimes pretended a fondness for him, but Ming always moved gracefully but unmistakably in another direction.

Ming's nap was interrupted by the sound of the cabin door opening. He heard Elaine and the man laughing and talking. The big red-orange sun was near the horizon.

'Ming!' Elaine came over to him. 'Aren't you getting *cooked*, darling? I thought you were *in*!'

'So did I!' said Teddie.

Ming purred as he always did when he awakened. She picked him up gently, cradled him in her arms, and took him below into the suddenly cool shade of the cabin. She was talking to the man, and not in a gentle tone. She set Ming down in front of his dish of water, and though he was not thirsty, he drank a little to please her. Ming did feel addled by the heat, and he staggered a little.

Elaine took a wet towel and wiped Ming's face, his ears and his four paws. Then she laid him gently on the bunk that smelled of Elaine's perfume but also of the man whom Ming detested.

Now his mistress and the man were quarrelling, Ming could tell from the tone. Elaine was staying with Ming, sitting on the edge of the bunk. Ming at last heard the splash that meant Teddie had dived into the water. Ming hoped he stayed there, hoped he drowned, hoped he never came back. Elaine wet a bathtowel in the aluminium sink, wrung it out, spread it on the bunk, and lifted Ming on to it. She brought water, and now Ming was thirsty, and drank. She left him to sleep again while she washed and put away the dishes. These were comfortable sounds that Ming liked to hear.

But soon there was another *plash* and *plop,* Teddie's wet feet on the deck, and Ming was awake again.

The tone of quarrelling recommenced. Elaine went up the few steps on to the deck. Ming, tense but with his chin still resting on the moist bathtowel, kept his eyes on the cabin door. It was Teddie's feet that he heard descending. Ming lifted his head slightly, aware that there was no exit behind him, that he was trapped in the cabin. The man paused with a towel in his hands, staring at Ming.

Ming relaxed completely, as he might do preparatory to a yawn, and this caused his eyes to cross. Ming then let his tongue slide a little way out of his mouth. The man started to say something, looked as if he wanted to hurl the wadded towel at Ming, but he wavered, whatever he had been going to say never got out of his mouth, and he threw the towel in the sink, then bent to wash his face. It was not the first time Ming had let his tongue slide out at Teddie. Lots of people laughed when Ming did this, if they were people at a party, for instance, and Ming rather enjoyed that. But Ming sensed that Teddie took it as a hostile gesture of some kind, which was why Ming did it deliberately to Teddie, whereas among other people, it was often an accident when Ming's tongue slid out.

The quarrelling continued. Elaine made coffee. Ming began to feel better, and went on deck again, because the sun had now set. Elaine had started the motor, and they were gliding slowly towards the shore. Ming caught the song of birds, the odd screams, like shrill phrases, of certain birds that cried only at sunset. Ming looked forward to the adobe house on the cliff that was his and his mistress's home. He knew that the reason she did not leave him at home (where he would have been more comfortable) when she went on the boat, was because she was afraid that people might trap him, even kill him. Ming understood. People had tried to grab him from almost under Elaine's eyes. Once he had been suddenly hauled away in a cloth bag and, though fighting as hard as he could, he was not sure he would have been able to get out if Elaine had not hit the boy herself and grabbed the bag from him.

Ming had intended to jump up on the cabin roof again but, after glancing at it, he decided to save his strength, so he crouched on the warm, gently sloping deck with his feet tucked in, and gazed at the approaching shore. Now he could hear guitar music from the beach. The voices of his mistress and the man had come to a halt. For a few moments, the loudest sound was the *chug-chug-chug* of the boat's motor. Then Ming heard the man's bare feet climbing the cabin steps. Ming did not turn his head to look at him, but his ears twitched back a little, involuntarily. Ming looked at the water just the distance of a short leap in front of him and below him. Strangely, there was no sound from the man behind him. The hair on Ming's neck prickled, and Ming glanced over his right shoulder.

At that instant, the man bent forward and rushed at Ming with his arms outspread.

Ming was on his feet at once, darting straight towards the man, which was the only direction of safety on the rail-less deck, and the man swung his left arm and cuffed Ming in the chest. Ming went flying backward, claws scraping the deck, but his hind legs went over the edge. Ming clung with his front feet to the sleek wood which gave him little hold, while his hind legs worked to heave him up, worked at the side of the boat which sloped to Ming's disadvantage.

The man advanced to shove a foot against Ming's paws, but Elaine came up the cabin steps just then.

'What's happening? *Ming!*'

Ming's strong hind legs were getting him on to the deck little by little. The man had knelt as if to lend a hand. Elaine had fallen on to her knees also, and had Ming by the back of the neck now.

Ming relaxed, hunched on the deck. His tail was wet.

'He fell overboard!' Teddie said. 'It's true, he's groggy. Just lurched over and fell when the boat gave a dip.'

'It's the sun. Poor *Ming!*' Elaine held the cat against her breast, and carried him into the cabin. 'Teddie – could you steer?'

The man came down into the cabin. Elaine had Ming on the bunk and was talking softly to him. Ming's heart was still beating fast. He was alert against the man at the wheel, even though Elaine was with him. Ming was aware that they had entered the little cove where they always went before getting off the boat.

Here were the friends and allies of Teddie, whom Ming detested by association, although these were merely Mexican boys. Two or three boys in shorts called 'Señor Teddie!' and offered a hand to Elaine to climb on to the dock, took the rope attached to the front of the boat, offered to carry '*Ming! – Ming!*' Ming leapt on to the dock himself and crouched, waiting for Elaine, ready to dart away from any other hand that might reach for him. And there were several brown hands making a rush for him, so that Ming had to keep jumping aside. There were laughs, yelps, stomps of bare feet on wooden boards. But there was also the reassuring voice of Elaine warning them off. Ming knew she was busy carrying off the plastic satchels, locking the cabin door. Teddie with the aid of one of the Mexican boys was stretching the canvas over the cabin now. And Elaine's sandalled feet were beside Ming. Ming followed her as she walked away. A boy took the things Elaine was carrying, then she picked Ming up.

They got into the big car without a roof that belonged to Teddie, and drove up the winding road towards Elaine's and Ming's house. One of the boys was driving. Now the tone in which Elaine and Teddie were speaking was calmer, softer. The man laughed. Ming sat tensely on his mistress's lap. He could feel her concern for him in the way she stroked him and touched the back of his neck. The man reached out to put his fingers on Ming's back, and Ming gave a low growl that rose and fell and rumbled deep in his throat.

'Well, well,' said the man, pretending to be amused, and took his hand away.

Elaine's voice had stopped in the middle of something she was saying. Ming was tired, and wanted nothing more than to take a nap on the big bed at home. The bed was covered with a red and white striped blanket of thin wool.

Hardly had Ming thought of this, when he found himself in the cool, fragrant atmosphere of his own home, being lowered gently on to the bed with the soft woollen cover. His mistress kissed his cheek, and said something with the word hungry in it. Ming understood, at any rate. He was to tell her when he was hungry.

Ming dozed, and awakened at the sound of voices on the terrace a couple of yards away, past the open glass doors. Now it was dark. Ming could see one end of the table, and could tell from the quality of the light that there were candles on the table. Concha, the servant who slept in the house, was clearing the table. Ming heard her voice, then the voices of Elaine and the man. Ming smelled cigar smoke. Ming jumped to the floor and sat for a moment looking out of the door towards the terrace. He yawned, then arched his back and stretched, and limbered up his muscles by digging his claws into the thick straw carpet. Then he slipped out to the right of the terrace and glided silently down the long stairway of broad stones to the garden below. The garden was like a jungle or a forest. Avocado trees and mango trees grew as high as the terrace itself, there were bougainvillaea against the wall, orchids in the trees, and magnolias and several camellias which Elaine had planted. Ming could hear birds twittering and stirring in their nests. Sometimes he climbed trees to get at their nests, but tonight he was not in the mood, though he was no longer tired. The voices of his mistress and the man disturbed him. His mistress was not a friend of the man's tonight, that was plain.

Concha was probably still in the kitchen, and Ming decided to go in and ask her for something to eat. Concha liked him. One maid who had not liked him had been dismissed by Elaine. Ming thought he fancied barbecued pork. That was what his mistress and the man had eaten tonight. The breeze blew fresh from the ocean, ruffling Ming's fur slightly. Ming felt completely recovered from the awful experience of nearly falling into the sea.

Now the terrace was empty of people. Ming went left, back into the bedroom, and was at once aware of the man's presence, though there was no light on and Ming could not see him. The man was standing by the dressing table, opening a box. Again involuntarily Ming gave a low growl which rose and fell, and Ming remained frozen in the position he had been in when he first became aware of the man, his right front paw extended for the next step. Now his ears were back, he was prepared to spring in any direction, although the man had not seen him.

'*Ssss-st!* Damn you!' the man said in a whisper. He stamped his foot, not very hard, to make the cat go away.

Ming did not move at all. Ming heard the soft rattle of the white necklace which belonged to his mistress. The man put it into his pocket, then moved to Ming's right, out of the door that went into the big living-room. Ming now heard the clink of a bottle against glass, heard liquid being poured. Ming went through the same door and turned left towards the kitchen.

Here he miaowed, and was greeted by Elaine and Concha. Concha had her radio turned on to music.

'Fish? – Pork. He likes pork,' Elaine said, speaking the odd form of words which she used with Concha.

Ming, without much difficulty, conveyed his preference for pork, and got it. He fell to with a good appetite. Concha was exclaiming 'Ah-eee-ee!' as his mistress spoke with her, spoke at length. Then Concha bent to stroke him, and Ming put up with it, still looking down at his plate, until she left off and he could finish his meal. Then Elaine left the kitchen. Concha gave him some of the tinned milk, which he loved, in his now empty saucer, and Ming lapped this up. Then he rubbed himself against her bare leg by way of thanks and went out of the kitchen, made his way cautiously into the living-room en route to the bedroom. But now Elaine and the man were out on the terrace. Ming had just entered the bedroom, when he heard Elaine call:

'Ming? Where are you?'

Ming went to the terrace door and stopped, and sat on the threshold.

Elaine was sitting sideways at the end of the table, and the candlelight was bright on her long fair hair, on the white of her trousers. She slapped her thigh, and Ming jumped on to her lap.

The man said something in a low tone, something not nice.

Elaine replied something in the same tone. But she laughed a little.

Then the telephone rang.

Elaine put Ming down, and went into the living-room towards the telephone.

The man finished what was in his glass, muttered something at Ming, then set the glass on the table. He got up and tried to circle Ming, or to get him towards the edge of the terrace, Ming realized, and Ming also realized that the man was drunk – therefore moving slowly and a little clumsily. The terrace had a parapet about as high as the man's hips, but it was broken by grilles in three places, grilles with bars wide enough for Ming to pass through, though Ming never did, merely looked through the grilles sometimes. It was plain to Ming that the man wanted to drive him through one of the grilles, or grab him and toss him over the terrace parapet. There was nothing easier for Ming than to elude him. Then the man picked up a chair and swung it suddenly, catching Ming on the hip. That had been quick, and it hurt. Ming took the nearest exit, which was down the outside steps that led to the garden.

The man started down the steps after him. Without reflecting, Ming dashed back up the few steps he had come, keeping close to the wall which was in shadow. The man hadn't seen him, Ming knew. Ming leapt to the terrace parapet, sat down and licked a paw once to recover and collect himself. His heart beat fast as if he were in the middle of a fight. And hatred ran in his veins. Hatred burned his eyes as he crouched and listened to the man uncertainly climbing the steps below him. The man came into view.

Ming tensed himself for a jump, then jumped as hard as he could, landing with all four feet on the man's right arm near the shoulder. Ming clung to the cloth of the man's white jacket, but they were both falling. The man groaned. Ming hung on. Branches crackled. Ming could not tell up from down. Ming jumped off the man, became aware of direction and of the earth too late, and landed on his side. Almost at the same time, he heard the thud of the man hitting the ground, then of his body rolling a little way, then there was silence. Ming had to breathe fast with his mouth open until his chest stopped hurting. From the direction of the man, he could smell drink, cigar, and the sharp odour that meant fear. But the man was not moving.

Ming could now see quite well. There was even a bit of moonlight. Ming headed for the steps again, had to go a long way through the bush, over stones and sand, to where the steps began. Then he glided up and arrived once more upon the terrace.

Elaine was just coming on to the terrace.

'Teddie?' she called. Then she went back into the bedroom where she turned on a lamp. She went into the kitchen. Ming followed her. Concha had left the light on, but Concha was now in her own room, where the radio played.

Elaine opened the front door.

The man's car was still in the driveway, Ming saw. Now Ming's hip had begun to hurt, or now he had begun to notice it. It caused him to limp a little. Elaine noticed this, touched his back, and asked him what was the matter. Ming only purred.

'Teddie? – Where are you?' Elaine called.

She took a torch and shone it down into the garden, down among the great trunks of the avocado trees, among the orchids and the lavender and pink blossoms of the bougainvillaeas. Ming, safe beside her on the terrace parapet, followed the beam of the torch with his eyes and purred with content. The man was not below here, but below and to the right. Elaine went to the terrace steps and carefully, because there was no rail here, only broad steps, pointed the beam of the light downward. Ming did not bother looking. He sat on the terrace where the steps began.

'Teddie!' she said. '*Teddie!*' Then she ran down the steps.

Ming still did not follow her. He heard her draw in her breath. Then she cried:

'*Concha!*'

Elaine ran back up the steps.

Concha had come out of her room. Elaine spoke to Concha. Then Concha became excited. Elaine went to the telephone, and spoke for a short while, then she and Concha went down the steps together. Ming settled himself with his paws tucked under him on the terrace, which was still faintly warm from the day's sun. A car arrived. Elaine came up the steps, and went and opened the front door. Ming kept out of the way on the terrace, in a shadowy corner, as three or four strange men came out on the terrace and tramped down the steps. There was a great deal of talk below, noises of feet, breaking of bushes, and then the smell of all of them mounted the steps, the smell of tobacco, sweat, and the familiar smell of blood. The man's blood. Ming was pleased, as he was pleased when he killed a bird and created this smell of blood under his own teeth. This was big prey. Ming, unnoticed by any of the others, stood up to his full height as the group passed with the corpse, and inhaled the aroma of his victory with a lifted nose.

Then suddenly the house was empty. Everyone had gone, even

Concha. Ming drank a little water from his bowl in the kitchen, then went to his mistress's bed, curled against the slope of the pillows, and fell fast asleep. He was awakened by the *rr-rr-r* of an unfamiliar car. Then the front door opened, and he recognized the step of Elaine and then Concha. Ming stayed where he was. Elaine and Concha talked softly for a few minutes. Then Elaine came into the bedroom. The lamp was still on. Ming watched her slowly open the box on her dressing table, and into it she let fall the white necklace that made a little clatter. Then she closed the box. She began to unbutton her shirt, but before she had finished, she flung herself on the bed and stroked Ming's head, lifted his left paw and pressed it gently so that the claws came forth.

'Oh, Ming – Ming,' she said.

Ming recognized the tones of love.

NOTES

Ming
> a name often given to a Siamese cat, a breed (from Siam, now Thailand) which is cream-coloured with a brown face and ears, and blue eyes

Acapulco (p110)
> a popular seaside resort and sea-port in Mexico

DISCUSSION

1 There are two dramas in this story: the interaction between Ming and the humans, and the interaction between the two humans, Elaine and Teddie. Did you find one more interesting than the other? Do you think the two dramas have equal weight in the story? How do they connect? Is one dependent on the other, or could they stand independently?

2 The story is told with a third-person narrator but the point of view is exclusively Ming's. Animal stories told in this way are sometimes anthropomorphic, in that the animals are given human characteristics or qualities. Is that the case here? Or do you feel Ming's thoughts and reactions are ones that could quite plausibly be attributed to a cat?

3 Does the author suggest that Ming is aware of the significance of the man putting the necklace into his pocket? And if so, do you think we are meant to interpret Ming's attack on Teddie as a response to this theft, an attempt to recover his mistress's property? Or are we meant to see Ming's actions solely as a primitive feline urge for revenge for the attacks Teddie had made on him? If this is the case, why was Teddie's theft of the necklace included in the story? What purpose does it serve?

4 Did you find the ending of the story satisfying? Did Teddie get what he deserved? In what other ways could the story have ended, and would these alternative endings have been more satisfying, or less?

5 There is a saying, 'Love me, love my dog', meaning that if you love someone, you must love everything that belongs to them. Suppose Teddie had been a loving partner, who disliked all cats intensely. What should Elaine, or indeed any fond cat owner, do in such a circumstance?

LANGUAGE FOCUS

1 This is Ming's story, Ming's version of events, but told in the third person. How different would it be if told in the first person? Try

rewriting the first paragraph of the story in the first person, as though Ming were telling the story to a friend. Then compare your version with the original. Which do you prefer, and why?

2   The author has observed cats very carefully, and these are some of the many words used to describe Ming's behaviour and movements. From this list choose ten or fifteen words which you think are particularly appropriate for describing a cat. Give reasons for your choice.

arch, climb, cling, crouch, dart, dash, dig, doze, glide, growl, heave, hunched, jump, leap, lick, lie, miaow, nap, purr, relaxed, rub, scrape, spring, squirm, step, stretch, tense, tuck, twitch, yawn

ACTIVITIES

1   In this story we are given the sense or the tone of the human conversations, as perceived by Ming, but rarely the actual words. Do you think this tends to distance the reader from the human characters, and if so, does this make the story more effective, or less?

Find these extracts in the text, and invent appropriate remarks or dialogue to fit the story at that point. What, in your opinion, would be the effect of including dialogue like this in the story?

* *Sometimes Teddie . . . muttered something which Ming knew was a threat.* (p112)
* *She was talking to the man, and not in a gentle tone.* (p112)
* *The man started to say something, looked as if he wanted to hurl the wadded towel at Ming . . .* (p113)
* *Elaine had Ming on the bunk and was talking softly to him.* (p115)
* *Concha was exclaiming 'Ah-eee-ee!' as his mistress spoke with her, spoke at length.* (p117)
* *The man said something in a low tone, something not nice. Elaine replied something in the same tone. But she laughed a little.* (p118)
* *The man finished what was in his glass, muttered something at Ming, then set the glass on the table.* (p118)
* *Elaine spoke to Concha. Then Concha became excited.* (p120)
* *Elaine and Concha talked softly for a few minutes.* (p121)

2   What do you imagine Elaine was thinking when she stroked Ming's head at the end of the story? Write her diary for that day. Is there any suggestion in the story that she is aware Ming caused Teddie's death?

THE CHILDREN

THE AUTHOR

John Morrison was born in the north of England in 1904, and emigrated to Australia in 1923. He was a basic wage earner all his life and wrote in his spare time, using his work experiences in the bush, as a council worker, and on the Melbourne waterfront as background for his stories. A socialist by conviction and a member of the Realist Writers Group, Morrison published his first short stories in trade union magazines. He went on to publish novels, *Port of Call* and *Creeping City*, but is probably best known for his fine collections of short stories, including *Sailors Belong Ships, Black Cargo, Twenty-Three, North Wind, Stories of the Waterfront*, and *This Freedom*. He was awarded the Gold Medal of the Australian Literature Society for *Twenty-Three*, and in 1986 received the Patrick White Award. He died in 1998.

THE STORY

There are some decisions that we all fervently hope we never have to make – terrifying decisions, impossible decisions, decisions that are made in the flick of an eye but which carry a lifetime's burden. And when the die is cast there is no turning back; the saddest words in the English language are 'if only'.

Mr Allen is leaving town. His lifetime's burden is now etched on his face, in his bloodshot eyes, his fire-scarred clothes. Around him lies the desolation caused by the forest fire that has swept through his local community. As he tightens a rope on his truck, he watches with hostile eyes the approach of yet another newspaperman, wanting yet more morbid details . . .

The Children

He was almost ready to go when I found him. He was, to be exact, engaged in putting the final lashings onto his big truck. Blackened and blistered, and loaded up with all his worldly possessions, it was backed right up to a dry old verandah littered with dead leaves and odds and ends of rubbish. He turned to me as I got near, his bloodshot eyes squinting at me with frank hostility.

'Another newshawk.'

'The *Weekly*, Mr Allen.'

His expression softened a little. 'I've got nothing against the *Weekly*.'

'We thought there might be something more to it,' I said gently. 'We know the dailies never tell a straight story.'

'They did this time,' he replied. 'I'm not making excuses.'

With the dexterity of a man who did it every day, he tied a sheepshank*, ran the end of the rope through a ring under the decking, up through the eye of the knot, and back to the ring.

'I've got something to answer for all right,' he said with tight lips. 'But nobody need worry, I'll pay! I'll pay for it all the rest of my life. I'm that way now I can't bear the sight of my own kids.'

I kept silent for a moment. 'We understand that, Mr Allen. We just thought there might be something that hasn't come out yet.'

'No, I wouldn't say there's anything that hasn't come out. It's just that – well, people don't think enough, they don't think, that's all.'

He was facing me now, and looking very much, in his immobility, a part of the great background of desolation. The marks of fire were all over him. Charred boots, burned patches on his clothes, singed eyebrows, blistered face and hands, little crusts all over his hat where sparks had fallen. Over his shoulder the sun was just rising between Hunter and Mabooda Hills*, a monstrous ball of copper glowing and fading behind the waves of smoke still drifting up from the valley. Fifty yards away the dusty track marked the western limit of destruction. The ground on this side of it was the first brown earth I had seen since leaving Burt's Creek; Allen's house the first survivor after a tragic procession of stark chimney stacks and overturned water tanks.

'It must have been hell!' I said.

'That?' He made a gesture of indifference. 'That's nothing. It'll come good again. It's the children.'

'I know.'

The door of the house opened. I saw a woman with children at her skirts. She jumped as she caught sight of me, and in an instant the door banged, leaving me with an impression of whirling skirts and large frightened eyes.

'The wife's worse than me,' said Allen, 'she can't face anybody.'

He was looking away from me now, frowning and withdrawn, in the way of a man living something all over again, something he can't leave alone. I could think of nothing to say which wouldn't sound offensively platitudinous. It was the most unhappy assignment I had ever been given. I couldn't get out of my mind the hatred in the faces of some men down on the main road when I'd asked to be directed to the Allen home.

I took out my cigarettes, and was pleased when he accepted one. A man won't do that if he has decided not to talk to you.

'How did it come to be you?' I asked. 'Did Vince order you to go, or did you volunteer?' Vince was the foreman ranger in that part of the Dandenongs.

'I didn't ask him, if that's what you mean. I don't work for the Commission*. The truck's my living, I'm a carrier. But everybody's in on a fire, and Vince is in charge.'

'Vince picked you . . .'

'He picked me because I had the truck with me. I'd been down to the Gully to bring up more men, and it was parked on the break*.'

'Then it isn't true . . .'

'That I looked for the job because of my own kids? No! That's a damned lie. I didn't even have cause to be worried about my own kids just then. I'm not trying to get out of it, but there's plenty to blame besides me: the Forestry Commission, the Education Department and everybody in Burt's Creek and Yileena if it comes to that. Those children should never have been there to begin with. They should have been sent down to the Gully on Friday or kept in their homes. The fire was on this side of the reserve right up to noon.'

He wheeled, pointing towards the distant top of Wanga Hill. Through the drifting haze of smoke we could make out the little heap of ruins closely ringed by black and naked spars that had been trees. Here and there along the very crest, where the road ran, the sun glinted now and then on the windscreens of standing cars, morbid sightseers from the city.

'Just look at it!' he said vehemently. 'Timber right up to the fence-lines! A school in a half-acre paddock – in country like this!'

His arm fell. 'But what's the use of talking? I was told to go and get the kids out, and I didn't do it. I got my own. Nothing else matters now.'

'You thought there was time to pick up your own children first, and then go on to the school, Mr Allen?'

'That's about the size of it,' he assented gloomily.

I'd felt all along that he did want to talk to somebody about it. It came now with a rush.

'Nut it out* for yourself,' he appealed. 'What your paper says isn't going to make anybody think any different now. But I'll tell you this: there isn't another bloke in the world would have done anything else. I should be shot – I wish to God they would shoot me! – but I'm still no worse than anybody else. I was the one it happened to, that's all. Them people who lost kids have got a perfect right to hate my guts, but supposing it had been one of them? Supposing it had been you . . . what would you have done?'

I just looked at him.

'You know, don't you? In your own heart you know?'

'Yes, I know.'

'The way it worked out you'd think somebody had laid a trap for me. Vince had got word that the fire had jumped the main road and was working up the far side of Wanga. And he told me to take the truck and make sure the kids had been got away from the school. All right – now follow me. I get started. I come along the low road there. I get the idea right away that I'll pick up my own wife and kids afterwards. But when I reach that bit of open country near Hagen's bridge when you can see Wanga, I look up. And, so help me God! there's smoke. Now that can mean only one thing: that the Burt's Creek leg of the fire has jumped the Government break and is heading this way. Think that one over. I can see the very roof of my house, and there's smoke showing at the back of it. I know there's scrub right up to the fences, and I've got a wife and kids there. The other way there's twenty kids, but there's no smoke showing yet. And the wind's in the north-east. And I'm in a good truck. And there's a fair track right through from my place to the school. What would you expect me to do?'

He would see the answer in my face.

'There was the choice,' he said with dignified finality. 'One way, my own two kids. The other way, twenty kids that weren't mine. That's how everybody sees it, just as simple as that.'

'When did you first realise you were too late for the school?'

'As soon as I pulled up here. My wife had seen me coming and was outside with the kids and a couple of bundles. She ran up to the truck as I stopped, shouting and pointing behind me.' He closed his eyes and shivered. 'When I put my head out at the side and looked back I couldn't see the school. A bloke just above the creek had a lot of fern and blackberry cut, all ready for burning off. The fire had got into that and was right across the bottom of Wanga in the time it took me to get to my place from the road. The school never had a hope. Some of the kids got up as far as the road, but it's not very wide and there was heavy fern right out to the metal.'

I waited, while he closed his eyes and shook his head slowly from side to side.

'I'd have gone through, though, just the same, if it hadn't been for the wife. She'll tell you. We had a fight down there where the tracks branch. I had the truck flat out and headed for Wanga. I knew what it meant, but I'd have done it. I got it into my head there was nothing else to do but cremate the lot, truck and everything in it. But the wife grabbed the wheel. It's a wonder we didn't leave the road.'

'You turned back . . .'

'Yes, damn my soul! I turned back. There was fire everywhere. Look at the truck. The road was alight both sides all the way back to Hagen's. Just the same, it would have been better if we'd gone on.'

That, I felt, was the simple truth, his own two innocents notwithstanding. I had an impulse to ask him what happened when he reached Burt's Creek, but restrained myself. His shame was painful to witness.

A minute or two later I said goodbye. He was reluctant to take my hand.

'I kept trying to tell myself somebody else might have got the kids out,' he whispered. 'But nobody did. Word had got around somehow that the school had been evacuated. Only the teacher – they found her with a bunch of them half a mile down the road. And to top it all off my own place got missed! That bit of cultivation down there – you wouldn't read about it, would you?'

No, you wouldn't read about it.

In the afternoon, at the Gully, standing near the ruins of the hotel, I saw him passing. A big fire-scarred truck rolling slowly down the debris-littered road. Behind the dirty windscreen one could just discern the hunted faces of a man and woman. Two children peeped out of a torn side-curtain. Here and there people searching the ashes of their homes stood upright and watched with hard and bitter faces.

NOTES

sheepshank (p125)

a kind of knot, one used to shorten a rope temporarily

Hunter and Mabooda Hills, (also Burt's Creek, the Dandenongs, Yileena, the Gully, Wanga Hill) (p125)

local place names (the story is set in Australia, near Melbourne)

the Commission (p126)

short for Forestry Commission, which manages and looks after the country's forests

the break (the Government break) (p127)

a fire-break in a forest, a 'corridor' kept clear of trees and undergrowth in order to prevent a forest fire spreading to the next section of trees

nut it out (p127)

(Australian slang) think it out

DISCUSSION

1 Allen was not trying to excuse his own actions, but he said that there were also other people to blame. What examples did he give, and do you think that these were valid points to make?

2 Read again Allen's explanation to the reporter about the calculations he made concerning the progress of the fire. Is he suggesting, do you think, that the one and only factor which spoilt his calculations was the cut fern and blackberry, all ready for burning off – which presumably is *'that bit of cultivation'* he refers to later? Why does he say *'you wouldn't read about it, would you?'*, and why does the reporter agree with him?

3 During the interview Allen says to the reporter, *'Supposing it had been you . . . what would you have done? You know, don't you? In your own heart you know?'* How did you interpret the reporter's answer? How would *you* answer the question? Do you agree that everybody, in their 'own heart', would give the same answer?

4 When Allen tells the reporter that he thinks it would have been better if they had driven on and cremated the truck and everything in it, the reporter seems to agree with him. What is your opinion on that?

LANGUAGE FOCUS

1 When gathering information, a reporter usually asks a lot of questions, but how many questions does this reporter actually ask? What effect can a lot of questions have? Look at these two utterances by the reporter:

'We thought there might be something more to it.'

'It must have been hell!'

How different would the effect be if questions like these were asked:

'Is there anything else that you can tell us?'

'What was it like?'

Later, the reporter says to Allen, *'Then it isn't true . . .'* Compare the effect of this with the questions *'Is it true . . .?'* or *'Isn't it true . . .?'* Now look at the reporter's other utterances and try to analyse their probable effect on the listener in this context.

2 *A minute or two later I said goodbye. He was reluctant to take my hand.* What is the significance of 'reluctant' here?

3 Find these phrases and idiomatic expressions in the text, and rephrase them in your own words.

I've got nothing against the Weekly.   (p125)

We know the dailies never tell a straight story.   (p125)

I'm that way now I can't bear the sight of my own kids.   (p125)

It'll come good again.   (p126)

. . . which wouldn't sound offensively platitudinous.   (p126)

But everybody's in on a fire . . .   (p126)

I'm not trying to get out of it . . .   (p127)

That's about the size of it.   (p127)

I had the truck flat out and headed for Wanga.   (p129)

And to top it all off my own place got missed!   (p129)

ACTIVITIES

1 Write a short report for one of the daily newspapers that 'never tell a straight story'. Make it very critical of Allen, presenting the story as just a simple moral choice between his own kids and other people's kids.

2 Now write the report for the *Weekly*, using a concise and simple version of the information that Allen gave you. While not minimizing the tragedy in any way, try also to express sympathy for Allen's terrible dilemma and to hint that every father in the world would probably have done the same thing.

MABEL

THE AUTHOR

William Somerset Maugham was born in 1874. He originally qualified as a doctor but soon became a full-time writer of plays, short stories, and novels. In both world wars he served as a British Intelligence agent, and travelled widely in the South Seas, south-east Asia, China, and Mexico. Many of his experiences in these places were later incorporated into his stories. His most famous novels are *Of Human Bondage*, *The Moon and Sixpence*, *Cakes and Ale*, and *The Razor's Edge*. His short stories have been published in various collections, and include some that have been considered among the best in the language, such as 'Rain' and 'The Alien Corn'. Many have been made into films or plays for the theatre. Maugham died in 1965.

THE STORY

Shakespeare, like many other poets, wrote a great deal on the subject of love. One of his most famous sonnets opens with these lines:

> Let me not to the marriage of true minds
> Admit impediments. Love is not love
> Which alters when it alteration finds . . .

That might not always be true in practice, but it is certainly a fine and noble sentiment.

In the days of the British Empire a young man called George paces the quayside in Rangoon, Burma, nervously awaiting the arrival of his bride-to-be from England. He and Mabel have been engaged for years, but at a distance of six thousand miles, and George suddenly gets cold feet. Mabel, however, is a remarkable woman, and more than equal to any impediments she might encounter . . .

MABEL

I was at Pagan, in Burma*, and from there I took the steamer to Mandalay, but a couple of days before I got there, when the boat tied up for the night at a riverside village, I made up my mind to go ashore. The skipper told me that there was a pleasant little club* in which I had only to make myself at home; they were quite used to having strangers drop off like that from the steamer, and the secretary was a very decent chap; I might even get a game of bridge. I had nothing in the world to do, so I got into one of the bullock-carts that were waiting at the landing-stage and was driven to the club. There was a man sitting on the veranda and as I walked up he nodded to me and asked whether I would have a whisky and soda or a gin and bitters. The possibility that I would have nothing at all did not even occur to him. I chose the longer drink and sat down. He was a tall, thin, bronzed man, with a big moustache, and he wore khaki shorts and a khaki shirt. I never knew his name, but when we had been chatting a little while another man came in who told me he was the secretary, and he addressed my friend as George.

'Have you heard from your wife yet?' he asked him.

The other's eyes brightened.

'Yes, I had letters by this mail. She's having no end of a time.'

'Did she tell you not to fret?'

George gave a little chuckle, but was I mistaken in thinking that there was in it the shadow of a sob?

'In point of fact she did. But that's easier said than done. Of course I know she wants a holiday, and I'm glad she should have it, but it's devilish hard on a chap.' He turned to me. 'You see, this is the first time I've ever been separated from my missus, and I'm like a lost dog without her.'

'How long have you been married?'

'Five minutes.'

The secretary of the club laughed.

'Don't be a fool, George. You've been married eight years.' After we had talked for a little, George, looking at his watch said he must go and change his clothes for dinner and left us. The secretary watched him disappear into the night with a smile of not unkindly irony.

'We all ask him as much as we can now that he's alone,' he told me. 'He mopes so terribly since his wife went home.'

'It must be very pleasant for her to know that her husband is as devoted to her as all that.'

'Mabel is a remarkable woman.'

He called the boy and ordered more drinks. In this hospitable place they did not ask you if you would have anything; they took it for granted. Then he settled himself in his long chair and lit a cheroot. He told me the story of George and Mabel.

They became engaged when he was home on leave, and when he returned to Burma it was arranged that she should join him in six months. But one difficulty cropped up after another; Mabel's father died, the war came, George was sent to a district unsuitable for a white woman, so that in the end it was seven years before she was able to start. He made all arrangements for the marriage, which was to take place on the day of her arrival, and went down to Rangoon to meet her. On the morning on which the ship was due he borrowed a motor-car and drove along to the dock. He paced the quay.

Then, suddenly, without warning, his nerve failed him. He had not seen Mabel for seven years. He had forgotten what she was like. She was a total stranger. He felt a terrible sinking in the pit of his stomach and his knees began to wobble. He couldn't go through with it. He must tell Mabel that he was very sorry, but he couldn't, he really couldn't marry her. But how could a man tell a girl a thing like that when she had been engaged to him for seven years and had come six thousand miles to marry him? He hadn't the nerve for that either. George was seized with the courage of despair. There was a boat at the quay on the very point of starting for Singapore; he wrote a hurried letter to Mabel, and without a stick of luggage, just in the clothes he stood up in, leaped on board.

The letter Mabel received ran somewhat as follows:

Dearest Mabel,

I have been suddenly called away on business and do not know when I shall be back. I think it would be much wiser if you returned to England. My plans are very uncertain. Your loving George.

But when he arrived at Singapore he found a cable waiting for him.

QUITE UNDERSTAND. DON'T WORRY. LOVE. MABEL.

Terror made him quick-witted.

'By Jove, I believe she's following me,' he said.

He telegraphed to the shipping-office at Rangoon and sure enough her name was on the passenger list of the ship that was now on its way to Singapore. There was not a moment to lose. He jumped on the train to Bangkok. But he was uneasy; she would have no difficulty in finding out that he had gone to Bangkok and it was just as simple for her to take the train as it had been for him. Fortunately there was a French tramp* sailing next day for Saigon*. He took it. At Saigon he would be safe; it would never occur to her that he had gone there; and if it did, surely by now she would have taken the hint. It is five days' journey from Bangkok to Saigon and the boat is dirty, cramped, and uncomfortable. He was glad to arrive and took a rickshaw to the hotel. He signed his name in the visitors' book and a telegram was immediately handed to him. It contained but two words: *Love. Mabel.* They were enough to make him break into a cold sweat.

'When is the next boat for Hong-Kong?' he asked. Now his flight grew serious. He sailed to Hong-Kong, but dared not stay there; he went to Manila; Manila was ominous; he went on to Shanghai: Shanghai was nerve-racking; every time he went out of the hotel he expected to run straight into Mabel's arms; no, Shanghai would never do. The only thing was to go to Yokohama. At the Grand Hotel at Yokohama a cable awaited him:

SO SORRY TO HAVE MISSED YOU AT MANILA.
LOVE. MABEL.

He scanned the shipping intelligence* with a fevered brow. Where was she now? He doubled back to Shanghai. This time he went straight to the club and asked for a telegram. It was handed to him:

ARRIVING SHORTLY. LOVE. MABEL.

No, no, he was not so easy to catch as all that. He had already made his plans. The Yangtse is a long river and the Yangtse was falling. He could just about catch the last steamer that could get up to Chungking and then no one could travel till the following spring except by junk. Such a journey was out of the question for a woman alone. He went to Hankow and from Hankow to Ichang, he changed boats here and from Ichang through the rapids went to Chungking. But he was desperate now, he was not going to take any risks: there was a place called Cheng-tu, the capital of Szechuan, and it was four hundred miles away. It could only be reached by road, and the road was infested with brigands. A man would be safe there.

George collected chair*-bearers and coolies* and set out. It was with a sigh of relief that he saw at last the crenellated walls of the lonely Chinese city. From those walls at sunset you could see the snowy mountains of Tibet.

He could rest at last: Mabel would never find him there. The consul happened to be a friend of his and he stayed with him. He enjoyed the comfort of a luxurious house, he enjoyed his idleness after that strenuous escape across Asia, and above all he enjoyed his divine security. The weeks passed lazily one after the other.

One morning George and the consul were in the courtyard looking at some curios that a Chinese had brought for their inspection when there was a loud knocking at the great door of the Consulate. The door-man flung it open. A chair borne by four coolies entered, advanced, and was set down. Mabel stepped out. She was neat and cool and fresh. There was nothing in her appearance to suggest that she had just come in after a fortnight on the road. George was petrified. He was as pale as death. She went up to him.

'Hullo, George, I was so afraid I'd missed you again.'

'Hullo, Mabel,' he faltered.

He did not know what to say. He looked this way and that: she stood between him and the doorway. She looked at him with a smile in her blue eyes.

'You haven't altered at all,' she said. 'Men can go off so dreadfully in seven years and I was afraid you'd got fat and bald. I've been so nervous. It would have been terrible if after all these years I simply hadn't been able to bring myself to marry you after all.'

She turned to George's host.

'Are you the consul?' she asked.

'I am.'

'That's all right. I'm ready to marry him as soon as I've had a bath.'

And she did.

NOTES

Burma (p134)

the official name of Burma since 1989 is Myanmar

club (p134)

these were social clubs for the use of the British officers and administrators of the Empire, not for the local people of the country

a French tramp (p136)

tramp steamers were small cargo vessels that sailed between local ports

Saigon (p136)

now known as Ho Chi Minh City

intelligence (p137)

(old-fashioned) information, news

chair (p137)

this would have been a kind of sedan chair, an enclosed chair for one person, carried between horizontal poles by two or four porters

coolie (p137)

(old-fashioned) a word, now regarded as offensive, for an unskilled worker in Asian countries

DISCUSSION

1 Did you find this story amusing? Do you think it is a kind of 'happy-ever-after' fairy tale, a piece of light-hearted fun, or are there also some serious points being made about relationships? If so, what might they be?

2 Because of the way the story is told, we know at the beginning that there is a happy ending, in that George and Mabel have been a devoted married couple for eight years. Did knowing the ending spoil your enjoyment of the story or not? Can you think of any reasons why the author structured the story in this way?

LANGUAGE FOCUS

1 Rephrase these colloquial expressions in your own words:

She's having no end of a time. (p134)

. . . it's devilish hard on a chap. (p134)

He couldn't go through with it. (p135)

. . . no, Shanghai would never do. (p137)

Men can go off so dreadfully in seven years . . . (p138)

2   The expressions below convey some of the fear or panic that poor
    George experiences in his headlong flight. Are there any which you think
    are humorous in themselves, regardless of the context they are used in?
    Are all of them only suitable for use in a light-hearted context, or could
    some be used in a more serious situation? If so, which?

    His nerve failed him.
    He felt a terrible sinking in the pit of his stomach.
    His knees began to wobble.
    . . . he hadn't the nerve for that either.
    . . . he was uneasy.
    . . . enough to make him break into a cold sweat.
    Shanghai was nerve-racking . . .
    . . . with a fevered brow.
    George was petrified.
    He was as pale as death.

ACTIVITIES

1   The cable that George finds waiting for him at Singapore doesn't actually
    reply to what George wrote in his letter. It seems that Mabel read
    between the lines and answered the letter that George *didn't* write. Write
    the letter that George might have written if he had been braver, and
    which would match Mabel's answer.

2   Imagine that Mabel has an anxious mother back in England, waiting
    for news of her daughter's marriage. Write a series of cheerful,
    reassuring telegrams for Mabel to send from the various cities she visits
    in her pursuit of George. The final one, from Cheng-tu, could be a little
    longer than the others.

3   Before the secretary of the club begins the tale, we have the sentence
    He told me the story of George and Mabel. So why is the story not
    called *George and Mabel*? Why just *Mabel*? Invent some different titles
    for the story, perhaps suggesting the humorous element, or the love
    aspect, or the Far Eastern setting.

Questions for Discussion or Writing

1 Out of all the stories in this book, which character did you feel most sympathy for? Is that because you sympathized with their particular emotional predicament, or because you felt their sufferings were through no fault of their own, or for some other reason? Which character did you feel least sympathy for, and why?

2 Look at all the stories and decide if they are narrated mostly from a woman's or a man's point of view. Then see which stories have male or female authors. Is there any correlation? Are stories with female points of view written by female authors, and vice versa? Do you think it is possible, when writing about emotional relationships, for a male author to write convincingly from a female point of view, or a female author from a male point of view? Can you think of any examples from your reading where this has been done effectively?

3 Both *The Garden Party* and *Roman Fever* are partly about revenge. Compare the way these two stories deal with this theme. Are both treatments realistic in your view? Could you imagine people behaving like this in real life?

4 *Roman Fever* and *The Legacy* both deal with deception, followed by a revelation. Were the revelations handled in the same way – for example, did they both come like a bolt from the blue, or does the author give the reader hints as to what is coming? Which method is more effective in your opinion?

5 James Duffy in *A Painful Case* and Arthur Lawson in *The Kimono* are both offered the opportunity of relationships, and each responds differently. Did either of them make the right decision, in terms either of moral judgements or of their own emotional well-being? Would making the opposite decision have been more satisfactory for either of these men?

6　Look again at *A Shocking Accident*, *Horrors of the Road*, *Mabel*, and perhaps *Ming's Biggest Prey*. They all have elements of humour in them. Is it the same kind of humour in each story? How would you describe the differences? Did you find one of the stories more effective than the others? Did any of them make you actually laugh?

7　It is said that the most selfless love is that of a parent for a child. Do you agree with this? Does the story *The Children* support this view? Do any of the other stories provide examples of selfless love?

8　'Love comforteth like sunshine after rain,' wrote Shakespeare in his poem *Venus and Adonis*. Can you find any comfort in these stories, even if only small crumbs of comfort? Do you prefer love stories that end happily, or sadly? What is your favourite love story, whether told in a short story, a novel, a poem, a film, a play? What is it about this story that makes it memorable for you?

9　Shakespeare's *Venus and Adonis*, a love story from ancient Greek mythology, was a bestseller in its day, reprinting about fifteen times, and love stories – whether sad, happy, tragic, comic, romantic, or absurd – have been popular since story-telling began, back in the mists of time. Why do you think this is so?

10　Which of the stories in this book did you like best, and why? Which would you recommend to a friend? Write a short review of this story for a newspaper or a magazine.

11　Would any of the stories in this book make a good film? Choose one, and write a description – perhaps in the form of a proposal to a film company – of the kind of film you would make. Would you want to change any details to make the visual story-telling more effective? Select an important moment in your chosen story and write the screenplay for that scene, including directions for the actors.

FROM THE CRADLE TO THE GRAVE

Editor: Clare West

Short stories by

Evelyn Waugh, Somerset Maugham, Roald Dahl,Saki,
Frank Sargeson, Raymond Carver, H. E. Bates, Susan Hill

This collection of short stories explores the trials of life from youth to old age: the idealism of young people, the stresses and strains of marriage, the anxieties of parenthood, and the loneliness and fears of older people. The wide variety of writing styles includes black humour, satire, and compassionate and realistic observation of the follies and foibles of humankind.

CRIME NEVER PAYS

Editor: Clare West

Short stories by

Agatha Christie, Graham Greene, Ruth Rendell,
Angela Noel, Dorothy L. Sayers, Margery Allingham,
Sir Arthur Conan Doyle, Patricia Highsmith

Murder: the unlawful, intentional killing of a human being – a terrible crime. But murder stories are always fascinating. Who did it? And how? Or why? Was it murder at all, or just an unfortunate accident? Who will triumph, the murderer or the detective? This collection contains a wide range of murder stories, from the astute detection of the famous Sherlock Holmes, to the chilling psychology of Ruth Rendell.

A Window on the Universe

Editor: Jennifer Bassett

Short stories by

Ray Bradbury, Bill Brown, Philip K. Dick,
Arthur C. Clarke, Jerome Bixby, Isaac Asimov,
Brian Aldiss, John Wyndham, Roald Dahl

What does the future hold in store for the human race? Aliens from distant galaxies, telepathic horror, interstellar war, time-warps, the shriek of a rose, collision with an asteroid – the unknown lies around every corner, and the universe is a big place. These nine science-fiction stories offer possibilities that are fantastic, humorous, alarming, but always thought-provoking.

The Eye of Childhood

Editors: John Escott & Jennifer Bassett

Short stories by

John Updike, Graham Greene, William Boyd,
Susan Hill, D. H. Lawrence, Saki, Penelope Lively,
Bernard MacLaverty, Frank Tuohy, Morley Callaghan

What does it feel like to be a child? Learning how to negotiate with the unpredictable adult world, learning how to pick a path through life's traps and hazards, learning when the time has come to put away childish things. The writers of these short stories show us the world as seen from the far side of the child–adult divide, a gap that is sometimes small, and sometimes an unbridgeable chasm.